A GIFT OF HERBS

How to Make Easy, Inexpensive and Thoughtful Gifts Using Herbs

Heidi Hartwiger

Illustrated by Susan Tracy

 Down Home Press, Asheboro, N.C.

ISBN No. 1-878086-23-5

Library of Congress Catalog Card Number
93-071832

Printed in the United States of America

Cover design and illustrations: Susan Tracy
Book design: Elizabeth House

Down Home Press
P.O. Box 4126
Asheboro, N.C. 27204

Simple Gifts

'Tis the gift to be simple, 'tis the gift to be free,
'Tis the gift to come down where we ought to be.
And when we find ourselves in the place just right,
'Twill be in the valley of love and delight.
When true simplicity is gain'd,
To bow and to bend we shan't be ashamed,
To turn, turn will be our delight,
Till by turning, turning we come round right.
                                        ...A Shaker Hymn

*This book is dedicated
to "Sidney Dear"
who lit the spark
and to
"Aunt Janey" who fanned the flames.*

A special thank you goes to Jon Leeds, Martha Macdonald, Dot Jackson, the SELU Sisters, dear friends in the Appalachian Writers Association and my family who encouraged me to develop this project.

Contents

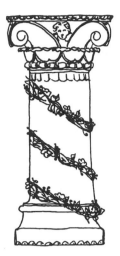

Herb
Folklore

Hold on a minute! Do you remember when you first heard about herbs?

Was it Shakespeare's Oberon and Titania leading you to a place where the wild thyme blows? In Bible stories at Sunday school? Latin I in ninth grade? In the garden at your granny's elbow? Maybe in a dish you tasted at a party and had to pledge secrecy to get the recipe. Think about it. If you weren't an herb lover or at least herb friendly, chances are you wouldn't be browsing through this book. So dear herb lover, welcome to the world of herbs as I have come to know them.

I would like to believe that somewhere at the dawn of civilization man walked through an herb meadow and, overcome by the fragrance, gathered an armload of aromatic plants to take home to woman. After she put some herbs in her hair, she used other herbs as nourishment. The remaining herbs she spread around the sleeping area and living quarters. A lovely pastoral picture. However, setting romantic notions aside, I've come to terms with the fact that herbs were used early on for their medicinal qualities. Historians agree the earliest collection of medicinal herbs was compiled in China around 2700 BC.

The Greeks and Romans used herbs for brewing, strewing, valor, and strength.

These ancients revered the religious significance of herbs through tributes and ceremonies to a variety of gods and goddesses. The Roman Goddess, Venus, is frequently associated with love and romance. Did you know the lovely Venus is also considered as the protector of the garden and the patroness of the rose and the apple?

Although she is considered a lesser goddess, Flora is often linked with Venus. Flora's major obligation was to oversee Adonis, Crocus and Narcissus and others who through unfortunate circumstances were changed into flowers, thus they had to call the garden "home." One story tells us that each time the beautiful goddess Flora brushed or shook her long, glorious hair, blossoms cascaded from it.

Verification of ancient medicinal interest in herbs comes from the writings of the Roman naturalist, Pliny the Elder (23-79 A.D.). Not only did Pliny translate the work of the Greek writers into Latin, but he also recorded many observations of creative experimental treatments involving use of medicinal properties in herbs and plants.

Through the centuries an emerging interest in herbs spurred on the compilation of many herbals. An herbal is a "be all, end all" book of herb information. In addition to Pliny, names such as Theophrasus, a Greek physician who studied with Aristotle, and Dioscorides, a physician educated in Greece who traveled with the Roman army, hold a special place in history and medical books.

Englishmen John Gerard and Nicholas Culpeper consistently appear and reappear as wellsprings of herbal information. Although used as a point of reference, Gerard was frequently criticized for inaccuracies. Culpeper, who came several centuries after Gerard, raised considerable controversy with his herbal. Historians indicate that Culpeper was a practicing astrologer as well as an herbalist. Consequently, all his herb theories and curative suggestions were rooted in large part in astrological folklore.

There are more, too numerous to mention, who have contributed through the centuries to create historical lore – from healing cures and warding off evil spirits to beauty enhancers and love potions.

Christianity was a beacon to brighten the Medieval horizon. The Christian church chased away the witches, spirits, sprites and every entity that had previously required a brew or potion to summon or suppress. The monks and priests saw to it that the pagan rituals were replaced with Christian rites. Mary, mother of Christ and embodiment of all that was pure and holy, symbolically became the rose, lily of the valley, rosemary and every other herb and flower assigned to Greek and Roman Goddesses.

Just as the monks controlled the mysteries of the church, they also controlled the secrets of the herbs. Within the walls of every monastery was a large herb garden. While the monks burned various herbs as incense, castle dwellers burned bay leaves, lavender and rosemary to keep the air disease free. Fresh air was dangerous. As plagues ravaged the cities and countryside, people, rich and poor, carried small clusters of fresh herbs and pomanders. As the poor approached what they considered a contaminated place with infection in the air, they sniffed the bouquet of herbs. The wealthy carried pomanders.

At first the pomanders were nothing more than oranges stuffed with spices. Although it was recognized that pomanders were a health necessity, eventually fashion influenced the way they were made. Little cases ornately designed of silver and other precious metals were filled with small balls of wax perfumed with exotic spices. These little cases – still within sniffing distance, were hung around the neck or pinned on as a brooch. It is reported that some gentlemen also had pomanders concealed in the heads of their walking sticks. Later it became fashionable to replace the perfumed wax with tiny vinegar-and-spice-soaked sponges.

In America's early days, herbs were a necessity of life. Every house had a kitchen herb garden. In addition to the culinary uses and medicinal purposes, herbs were tucked in storage areas to freshen garments, strewn on the floor to freshen the air and used as pesticides to keep fleas and other unwanted insect populations under control.

The colonial housewife also depended upon her garden for dyes. And when the tea was dumped in Boston harbor and no longer available/desirable, the ladies in the colonies turned to their gardens and brewed "Liberty Teas" from assorted herbs.

At Mount Vernon, near Alexandria, Virginia, George Washington planted a garden just under an acre in area with enough vegetables and herbs to satisfy the needs of the ninety people who lived there. Today the garden is maintained by The Mount Vernon Ladies Association. Outside of Charlottesville, Virginia is Thomas Jefferson's home, Monticello. In his 1000 foot kitchen garden Jefferson planted 26 varieties of herbs. Today, horticulturists maintain the grounds, gardens and herb garden in much the same manner as Jefferson did. In Yorktown, Virginia behind Lord Nelson's house is a small but charming herb garden planted and maintained by the local chapter of the Children of the American Revolution.

As the times changed, the focus changed for herbs. The emphasis was away from medicinal uses and toward fragrances. The 19th century women, American and European, became intrigued with fragrances and the symbolism in herbs and flowers. Relationships could be initiated or terminated according to the suggestion offered by an herbal bouquet. Elixirs laced with alcohol or opium obtained by prescription from doctors or purchased at traveling medicine shows replaced herbal remedies in many households. When the southern Atlantic coast was blockaded by the North during the Civil War, many southern women returned to the land for daily necessities. The humble dogwood became a toothbrush as twig ends were chewed to a delicate fray then rubbed on the teeth and gums to cleanse them.

Once again the focus has shifted to herbs. Today many people turn away from chemicals, preservatives and synthetics and return to the land, back to herbs for food, comfort and healing. It is not my intent to discuss the medicinal properties and curative powers of herbs. Rather, I want to share the simple pleasures I have discovered while working with herbs.

Dear herb lover, are you familiar with how something can be a part of your life before you realize it? I grew up with people for whom farming and honoring the land were a way of life. I took herbs for granted until I moved from West Virginia to eastern Virginia in the 1960's. At that point communes had sprung up on the west coast. Baking bread, eliminating preservatives and using herbs were viewed as really "far out." Those involved in such activities were carefully scrutinized by many, including the conventional folks living in this area peppered with military installations. Didn't alternative lifestyles somehow indicate subversion?

Still, in the populous tidewater area of Virginia I found I was surrounded by prestigious, historically correct 18th Century herb gardens, which meant an abundance of knowledgeable herb authorities. I toured herb gardens and snitched a leaf here and there, pressed it between my fingers, sighed at the fragrance. At the same moment I felt intimidated by the guides' seemingly endless wealth of information, I had a secret yearning to dwell among the herbs.

Meanwhile, in West Virginia my mother, unencumbered by "herban snobbery," cultivated her own herb garden. Between her and my best friend, Martha Macdonald, I caught herb fever. I began to read about herbs, but many of the books were so authoritative that again I backed away. It seemed as if there was a mysterious, elliptical network of knowledge. Not knowing how to enter the "charmed circle" of herb knowledge and being a distance from any of the communal lifestyles on the opposite coast, I ventured forth on my own. I did not have a trowel when I planted my first herb, a sage plant from

Martha. I dug the hole with a serving spoon. With that one plant, my herbal odyssey began.

I wish I could say I have a Biblical garden, a tea garden, or some intricately designed butterfly garden. Simply, I grow herbs wherever they are happiest in my yard.

My mother and I began culinary and craft experiments on family and friends with our herbs. This eventually developed into a small business. As she struggled with terminal cancer, my mother found great joy among her herbs. Although she was called home, she lives for me every time I brush against the thyme or see a bumble bee in the lemon balm. Because it is a joy, a simple pleasure for me, I feel a yoke of responsibility to expose as many people as I can to herb fever. It is highly contagious, and so rewarding.

This is a book for busy herb lovers. It is based on shortcuts I have devised over the years when I had too many children and never enough time or money. Let the perfectionists frown. Too bad! I am a non-traditional person so there are no long descriptions of how and where to plant herbs. This is not a botanical guide, nor does it burden you with horticultural directions. There's a plethora of books at your local library or bookseller offering such detail.

Before any "how-to" with herbs, I will acquaint you by means of folklore and historical trivia with most of the herbs mentioned in the book. Trivia is fun. Tense or boring moments can be lightened if you pepper your conversation with a little folklore, superstition, a quotation. Not to worry, busy herb lover, there will be a time to read in depth, but for now, how about a crash course?

Trivial Delights

(How to Combat Herban Snobbery)

BASIL – In some parts of the southwestern United States, it is thought that carrying basil in one's pocket will encourage wealth. It is reported that basil had its roots in India, was revered in households there and was sacrificed to Krishna and Vishnu. Ancient herbals recommend the use of basil for clearing out the head and also as a remedy for warts and worms. According to stories, the infamous Salome hid the severed head of John the Baptist in a pot of basil. John Keats perhaps saw basil as the source of Isabella's problems. In his poem, "Isabella," Keats made note that Isabella buried her dead lover's head in a pot of basil and watered it daily with her tears. Basil is one of those herbs, so legend has it, that was placed on the chest of the deceased as protection from evil in the next life and to offer swift entrance to heaven. Someone should have alerted the townsfolk of Salem, Massachusetts to this fact. Every Salem woman who was found to be growing basil in her garden was declared a witch.

CHAMOMILE – In Ancient Egypt chamomile was used for chills and other illnesses common to the times. Centuries later, Pliny reported

that chamomile in poultice form was good for
headaches, also kidney, bladder, and liver difficul-
ties. The medieval woman used this herb for strewing to keep the air fresh and the bugs away since it
is reported to have natural insect repellent qualities. Culpeper recommended bathing in a decoction of chamomile, which "taketh away weariness
and easeth pains and torments of the belly." After
Peter Rabbit feasted in Mr. Macgregor's garden, he

received chamomile tea from his mother. Through the centuries
blond and red haired women used chamomile as a rinse to highlight
their hair.

DILL – This herb was treasured for its charm qualities. As a medieval
charm, it could scare off witches and if carried in a bag
over the heart, could combat "evil eye." Because dill was
considered to have aphrodisiac qualities, it was an
important ingredient in love potions. Earlier in history
dill was used for its decorative value in Roman homes
and made into garlands to crown war heroes on their
return from battle. Dill water was given to restless babies
to put them into a peaceful sleep. Culpeper believed
that Mercury controlled this plant, therefore, dill
strengthened the brain. He also suggested boiling dill seeds in wine
then sniffing the potion to cure hiccups.

GARLIC – The ancients must have believed that garlic produced more
than bad breath. The Egyptians ate garlic cloves for strength while
building the pyramids. One story tells of the laborers refusing to work
until the daily garlic distribution. The Israelites ate garlic for
endurance in preparation for their exodus from Egypt. The followers
of Mohammed believe that garlic grew out of the ground where Satan
touched the ground with his left foot as he left the Garden of Eden
after man's fall. Since garlic belonged to Mars, the God of War,
Roman soldiers ate garlic for strength and courage before battling the
enemy. Garlic emerged in mythology as Odysseus used it against Circe
to prevent her from turning him into a pig. What worked for Odysseus
was tried in Medieval times. Garlic was used to protect against witches,
demons, and the ever present "evil eye." On the positive side, garlic
was recommended for its curative powers in matters of toothache, dog
bite, or poison arrow wounds. Garlic also was an important ingredient
in love potions. Even today in the United States, to combat trouble-
some worms and other intestinal parasites some mountain granny

women suggest eating a head of garlic everyday until the worms are gone.

LAVENDER – We've learned that in ancient times people bathed in herbal waters. It was recorded that Greeks and Romans scented their soaps and bathing water with lavender. In medieval times lavender was used as a strewing herb, as an aphrodisiac in love potions, and to cure such things as toothache, sore joints, and nervous palpitations. Culpepper suggested distilled lavender water applied to the nostrils reduced "tremblings and passions of the heart, and faintings and swoonings."

MARJORAM – In translation from ancient Greek this herb means "happiness." It is a delicate, aromatic herb used long ago to adorn  brides, grooms, and graves. It is thought that the Greeks planted marjoram on burial sites believing that the deceased would enjoy eternal rest and happiness. Mythology tells us that Aphrodite, the Greek Goddess of Love, was partial to marjoram. Evidently, Gerard looked on a decoction of marjoram as helpful when drunk by those who were given to "overmuch sighing." Centuries later Culpeper believed that marjoram, falling under the planet Mercury, strengthened the mind. He also recommended that marjoram juice be put in the ear to combat deafness, pain and roaring noise in the ear. Through history gentle marjoram was used as protection from witchcraft, as a strewing herb and for "swete" bags (sachets) and "swete washing water." At one point dairy farmers hung bunches of the herb in the barns to prevent the milk from curdling during thunderstorms. Being a mild flavored relative to oregano and sometimes confused with it by the ancients, marjoram is enjoyed for its culinary delights and is an integral part of potpourri and tussie-mussie bouquets.

MINT – A lovely nymph, Minthes, was the object of jealousy by Proserpina, wife of the underworld God, Pluto. As a result of Proserpina's wrath, Minthes was turned into a mint plant. In biblical times mint was referred to as one of the "bitter" herbs. It was recorded that the Pharisees paid their tithe with mint. The Hebrews spread mint on the floors of their temples. Since mint was mentioned so often in early English writings, more than likely it was brought by the Romans and was cultivated in monastery gardens for culinary and medicinal purposes. Many used it as a digestive aid, or as a refresher in bathwater. Because of its aroma mint was also a strewing herb. People used spearmint leaves to whiten their teeth. Culpeper cautioned on the use of mint since it is controlled by Venus, Roman Goddess of Love, it could stir up "bodily lust." Because mint was an important medicinal and culinary herb, the colonists brought rootings of mint to the new world.

PARSLEY – This herb moved in and out of favor through history. It was said the reason a parsley seed takes so long to start growing is that  it must make seven trips to the devil before it germinates. Supposedly, the Greeks fed parsley to their chariot horses before the races to encourage speed. After the race was won, the victory crowns were fashioned in part with parsley. The Greeks also spread parsley on the graves of the dead. The Romans put parsley to practical use, wearing it about the neck to protect against drunkenness. One medieval remedy for baldness was to sprinkle the affected head with parsley seeds before retiring for the night. In some areas of Pennsylvania gardeners will not have parsley growing in the house. They fear the plant will invite death into the household. A century ago Afro-Americans thought to transplant parsley would bring on illness or death.

ROSEMARY – Today, just as in the old days, a gift of rosemary indicates love, friendship, and remembrance. Translated from the Latin, rosemary means "dew of the sea." Students wore wreaths of rosemary while studying for final exams to promote good memory. Brides carried it at weddings and gave it to grooms to secure a long lasting relationship. Rosemary tossed into an open grave was a gesture to show the deceased would not be forgotten. Under a medieval pillow a sprig of rosemary would keep away witches and bad dreams because it was supposed to possess the powers of protection against the dark spirits. Burning rosemary branches in the 17th-Century English courts  of justice, protected the judge from plague, pestilence and other contaminations brought into the courtroom by the prisoners. The rosemary bush supposedly concealed Mary as she escaped with baby Jesus to Egypt. At one point she hung her cloak on a rosemary bush to dry. The flowers changed from white to blue and have remained blue to this day. As a result of the miraculous flower transformation, the plant was known from then on as "rose of Mary." Some say a rosemary bush will never exceed Christ's height nor live longer than 33 years, his age at death. If you grow rosemary, cultivate it well. A large healthy rosemary bush indicates a strong woman runs the household.

SAGE – No wonder sage has been popular since before recorded history. It is reported to prolong life and if sage thrives in the garden, prosperity is at hand for the household. As with rosemary, the healthier the sage, the stronger the woman of the house. Sage was placed in graves with rosemary to denote continued remembrance of the dead. Gerard believed that sage could stimulate the senses and increase memory. Robbers believed in the protective medicinal powers of sage. As protection when they entered and robbed the houses of those who had died of the plague, they mixed sage and twelve other herbs to make what came to be known as the Vinegar of the Four Thieves. Sage was one  of the herbs used in "handwashing water." The practical colonists used it for tea, tobacco, and hair rinse as well as for culinary needs. Sage and rue planted together in the garden will keep the toads away.

TANSY – As the myth goes, Zeus needed a cup-bearer. The handsome young man, Ganymede, was given tansy tea, became immortal and served Zeus for eternity. Although tansy, translated from Greek, means  immortality, its reputation is as a pesticide, especially potent in the battle against fleas. It was strewed with other aromatic herbs and also placed in caskets. Evidently the problem of fleas and indoor insects was omnipresent, so James II appointed a "royal herb strewer." This position eventually became a ceremonial one that included participation in royal coronations. Historians indicate that the last official recorded "Royal Herb Strewing" took place in 1820 at the coronation of George IV. Culpeper suggested a concoction of tansy to tighten loose teeth and another to remove freckles. After reports of toxic qualities when ingested, tansy's use as a culinary herb diminished; however, the button flowers are dried for decoration. In some mountain regions tansy is planted in orchards to keep pests away. Newly constructed beehives are rubbed with tansy leaves to encourage the bees into their new home.

THYME – In translation from Greek thyme as a noun means courage, as a verb it means to fumigate. Roman soldiers bathed in thyme water to increase energy, courage and strength. Pliny identified thyme as a  fumigant. In some castles thyme was burned to drive away stinging insects. Judges carried thyme into the courtroom to ward off pests and plague. Biblical students believe Mary mixed thyme with the hay in the manger bed of baby Jesus. Medieval ladies considered thyme symbolic of courage. They embroidered thyme and buzzing bees on scarves to send with their knights into tournaments and battle. Young girls carried thyme mixed in their bouquets hoping it would attract men. Culpeper recommended that thyme be taken internally for children with "chin-cough." When applied externally in a salve, thyme would cure warts and take away "hot swellings." Thyme use was recommended as a cure for bad dreams. To walk garden paths carpeted with thyme is to indulge the senses. Borders of thyme serve as home to birds and some believe, fairies. Shakespeare's mighty Oberon, King of the fairies, encouraged midsummer night revels in thyme-filled meadows.

"I know a bank where the wild thyme blows,
Where oxlips and the nodding violet grows,
Quite over-canopied with luscious woodbine,
With sweet-musk roses and with eglantine:"

A Midsummer's Night Dream,
Act II, Scene 1
William Shakespeare

Culinary Uses and Gifts

A word of caution: Although potentially toxic herbs are deliberately omitted from this book, some herbs may possess potent medicinal qualities and create undesirable side effects if taken in a highly concentrated form or in great quantity. So it is well to remember, as in all things, practice moderation especially when drinking herbal teas. On rare occasions a highly allergic person may develop a reaction when consuming quantities of herbal products. There can be dermatitis problems in handling a fresh herb such as rue. A person with skin sensitivities may develop a mild rash or itchy patches of skin. If any type of adverse reaction occurs, consult a physician.

Although there is some reference to herbal folklore throughout this volume, the book is not meant as a diagnostic, prescriptive handbook. The mission is to stimulate and encourage creative interest in simple-to-make herbal products for home pleasure or gift giving.

"And you may gather garlands there..."
Rokeby, Sir Walter Scott

Culinary Herbs

The culinary herbs selected for this list are with a few exceptions commonly used and therefore readily available in dried form on the shelves of local groceries, health and gourmet markets and surprisingly, in some large discount variety stores.Grocery stores in metropolitan areas carry a variety of fresh herbs in the produce department. If you catch herb fever, consider growing your own. Many annual herbs are easy to grow from seed in pots and window boxes, as well as small plots of ground. If the growing season is upon you, it is not too late. Annual as well as perennial plants are usually available at local nurseries or through the mail. At the end of this book you will find a list of fresh plant and dried herb sources.

The following list is composed of the most commonly used, readily available culinary herbs:

Basil	Mints (spearmint, peppermint)
Bay	Oregano
Chives	Parsley
Chamomile	Rosemary
Dill	Sage
Garlic	Savory
Geraniums (scented)	Tarragon
Lemon Balm	Thyme
Marjoram	Wild violets

A Short Vocabulary

Before realizing herbal culinary delights, the herb lover must understand a few key terms. Valuable time is saved if the reader has a working knowledge of terms before beginning a project. Be of good cheer, the vocabulary is at hand so there is no need to play flip-flop with a glossary.

BRUISE: A method to release herbal oils by gently crushing leaves and stems.

DECOCTION: A method to draw out the flavor of leaves, roots, seeds, and bark for teas and other herbal preparations. The ingredients are brought to a rolling boil then simmered for 15-20 minutes. The residue is strained before the tea is served.

INFUSION: Boiling water is poured over herbs and allowed to steep. Before the tea is consumed, the wilted herbs are removed by pouring through a strainer.

MORTAR AND PESTLE: A hard bowl and blunt end tool used to bruise, crush or grind herbs, seeds or other material.

SPRIG: A small cutting from an herb. Often used to garnish a plate, with iced drinks, or in vinegars and honey.

ZEST: Lemon, orange or other citrus peel scraped clean of the remaining rind.

Herbal Vinegars

Novice herb lovers need not be intimidated by gourmet chefs when preparing herbal vinegars. The two major requirements in vinegar preparation are that you be able to find your way to the kitchen and be willing to experiment. Rarely will you make a mistake with vinegars. Soon you will develop favorites, but for now, experiment, invent and enjoy the flavors. In this low fat, low cholesterol era you'll enjoy a guilt free, flavorful alternative in your diet. Herb sprigs in vinegar create a visually appealing gift. Who wouldn't appreciate a present with eye appeal and with practical use in salad dressings, for marinades, and any recipe that calls for vinegar?

Herb lovers are earth lovers, so as you recycle your glass bottles watch for 8 or 16-ounce bottles with character such as wine, spring water, salad dressing, olive oil or any other bottle with textured exterior and eye appeal. If you plan to use fresh herb sprigs, clear and lightly tinted bottles work well. The darker glass works for vinegar flavored with dry herbs. If you prefer to strain the herbs from the vinegar after it is flavored, the dark glass will do. Regardless of the type of bottle, you must remember to use a cork or plastic screw top. The acid in vinegar will react on metal caps without plastic liners. You can make a liner with a small protective piece of plastic wrap. Corks are available at hardware stores, craft shops and pharmacies.

LOVINGLY LONG PREPARATION: In this case "lovingly long" refers to aging time for the vinegar rather than actual preparation time.

Materials:
Clean bottle with stopper or top
Plastic funnel
Vinegar
Generous sprig of freshly cut, washed herb

Preparation:
Select vinegar according to preference. White vinegar is mild and allows the full flavor of the herb. This is important to remember when using the delicate thymes and basils. Rosemary, tarragon, sage and garlic are dominant flavors and will prevail in any type of vinegar. Vinegars other than white have flavorful characteristics that mix well with dominant herbs. Available vinegars are: White Cider, Wine (red and white) Malt (Note: For every eight ounces of vinegar use one large sprig of fresh herb or two tablespoons dried herb.)
Place a sprig of herb in a clean bottle.
Insert the funnel into the neck of the bottle.
Tilt the bottle slightly, gently pouring the vinegar into the funnel so the vinegar slides down the side of the bottle and doesn't crush the delicate herb.
Place cap on the bottle. Let vinegar stand in a warm place for four to six weeks. A window sill will do nicely, so you may enjoy looking at the sun doing its work on the vinegar.
To make a quantity of vinegar, use a large container and rebottle in smaller containers. This is your opportunity as you rebottle to strainthe vinegar if you choose to remove loose herbs.

Variations
VICTORIAN VIOLET VINEGAR
One half cup fresh violet leaves (washed)
One quart white vinegar or white wine vinegar
Process using herb vinegar directions.
This vinegar may be served as a refreshing cold beverage:
Dissolve three tablespoons of granulated sugar (or according to taste) in one cup water and add two or three (again, suit your taste) teaspoons of strained violet vinegar. Mix and pour over ice. Garnish with fresh violet flower or mint sprig.

Once you have mastered the single herb vinegars, try some blending herbs. Here are some suggestions to get you started. Why not create a kitchen specialty to give as gifts?
Hint 1: It is important when using fresh herbs in the vinegar to make sure the herbs are dry. If water mixes in with the vinegar, the result is cloudy vinegar. It is suitable for use, but not very attractive to view.
Hint 2: Consider using herbal vinegar in place of regular vinegar in your window washing water. As an alternative, mix the herb vinegar in with commercial pump bottle window wash solution. As the sun warms the window panes, a very subtle, clean aroma fills the air.

ROSEMARY AND GARLIC VINEGAR
4 tablespoons dried rosemary
2 cloves garlic
1 quart white vinegar

BASIL AND SUMMER SAVORY WINE VINEGAR
4 tablespoons dried, crumbled basil leaves
4 tablespoons dried crumbled summer savory
3 cloves garlic

DILL AND LEMON BALM WINE VINEGAR
1/2 cup fresh dill weed (4 tablespoons dry)
1/2 cup bruised lemon balm leaves (4 tablespoons dried)
1 quart white wine vinegar

BUSY HERB LOVER METHOD:
Determine the amount of vinegar you want to make and measure the ingredients.

Reserve a sprig of fresh herb.

Put the ingredients in a saucepan. (Ceramic, glass or stainless steel, not aluminum.)

Bring herbs and vinegar to just under a boil, reduce heat; cover and simmer for 15-20 minutes.

If you are decorating the vinegar with a fresh herb, let the vinegar cool before you add the herb. This is to prevent herb wilt.

Fill and seal the bottles as directed.

This vinegar is ready to use or give now.

Hint: It is a shame to wrap this gift. Tie a colorful bow around the neck of the bottle. To dress it up, melt paraffin or old candle stubs (busy herb lovers are often savers of things usable and questionable) in a double boiler. As the wax melts, color it with crayon shavings to accent the color of the bottle. (This is a good way to use crayon stubs. Don't mix too many colors, or the end result without fail will be army green!) Dip the top in the hot wax for an attractive seal. Repeat if a thick seal is desired.

Feeling Victorian? With velvet or satin ribbon tie a circle of lace over the cap.

"That's rosemary, that's for remembrance;
pray you, love, remember..."

Hamlet, Act IV, Scene V
William Shakespeare

Herbal Salts

With so many flavored salts available why make your own? It's fun, inexpensive, and easy. Many people who are cutting back on salt consumption reject traditional salt-free herb blends. As you venture into the world of herbal delights bringing somewhat reluctant friends and family members with you, comments such as, "Oh no, she's cooking with leaves again," or "There's something floating around in the soup," should not set you back. Be of good cheer! Herbal salts are a gentle transition, and the herbs are not visible. Remember, omit regular salt from your recipe if you are using an herbal salt.

The following herbs may be used individually or blended in any combination: Basil, bay leaf, chives, garlic, marjoram, oregano, rosemary, savory, tarragon, thyme.

LOVINGLY LONG METHOD:
Materials:
Baking pan (non-aluminum)
1 cup non-iodized salt
1 cup fresh herb or herb blend of choice
Air tight jar (RECYCLE! Use little jars in which dry herbs were packaged)

Preparation:
Chop fresh herb leaves. Combine herbs and salt. Crush the combination using mortar and pestle. Without mortar and pestle? Improvise and press the bottom of a heavy glass against the herbs in a sturdy bowl. Work the herbs into small bruised pieces. Spread crushed herbs and salt in the baking pan. Place in warm oven (200 degrees F). Check every 20 minutes and stir to break up lumps. Drying time is 45-60 minutes. For a finer texture use the mortar and pestle again. When herbal salt is cool, package in air tight containers, and store away from light.

Busy Herb Lover Method:
Use dry herbs instead of fresh.
Put dry herbs and salt in blender.
Whirl at medium speed for five seconds.
Check for desired consistency.If finer product is desired, whirl again.
Package as recommended.
Hint: As you grow bold with your mixtures, add a little lemon zest for tang or paprika for a rosy color. Dress up salt substitute with your herb blends for the mandatory salt free diets. You may make these far in advance because these blends stay fresh for many months.

Recipe Ideas:
Combine 1 teaspoon of the following dry herbs:
Marjoram
Basil
Bay leaf (one large)
Parsley
Table salt (non-iodized)
(One quarter-teaspoon of lemon zest is optional)

Poultry Salt
1 teaspoon lemon zest
2 teaspoons crushed dried marjoram
2 teaspoons crushed dried tarragon
1/4 cup non-iodized salt

Stuffing Seasoning for Poultry or Pork
2 teaspoons crumbled dried celery leaves
2 teaspoons crumbled dried parsley
2 teaspoons crumbled dried sage
1 teaspoon crumbled dried rosemary
1 teaspoon crumbled dried thyme
1/4 cup non-iodized salt

Beef Seasoning Salt
2 teaspoons crumbled dried celery leaves
2 teaspoons crumbled dried parsley
2 teaspoons crumbled dried summer savory
2 teaspoons crumbled dried thyme
1 bay leaf finely crumbled
1/4 cup non-iodized salt

Lamb Seasoning Salt
3 teaspoons finely crumbled dried rosemary
2 teaspoons crumbled dried thyme
1 teaspoon crushed dried lemon zest
1 teaspoon garlic powder
1/4 cup non-iodized salt

Variations to Use with Rice:
Tarragon Salt
2 teaspoons dried tarragon
2 teaspoons dried parsley flakes
1 teaspoon salt

4 tablespoons granulated chicken bouillon

Dill Salt

2 teaspoons dried minced chives
1 teaspoon salt
4 teaspoons dill seed
5 teaspoons dried grated lemon zest
2 tablespoons granulated chicken bouillon

Mix either the Tarragon or Dill Salt with four cups rice. Include favorite rice cooking directions.

Taco Seasoning

1/4 teaspoon dried oregano-
1/2 teaspoon instant minced garlic
1/4 teaspoon crushed dried red pepper
1/2 teaspoon cornstarch
1 teaspoon chili powder
1 teaspoon salt
2 teaspoons dry onion flakes

Pesto

Pesto is in a category all to itself, and it cannot in good conscience be overlooked. If you haven't experienced pesto and pasta now is the time. There is no substituting dry for fresh on this occasion. Haunt your grocery, gourmet market, trade something with your neighbor to get fresh basil and parsley. Rejoice, busy herb lover, this basil pesto recipe is enough for one pound of cooked spaghetti, fettuccine, or capellini, and it freezes beautifully.

Basil Pesto

2 cups firmly packed, bruised, shredded basil leaves
1/2 cups sprigs of parsley, stems cut in small sections
1/2 cup canola or olive oil
2 cloves crushed garlic
3 tablespoons finely chopped walnuts
1 teaspoon salt
Fill blender jar with all the ingredients. Blend at medium speed until ingredients form a thick puree. Stop the blender from time to time to scrape the splatters off the sides and back into the mixture. Be sure to use a rubber or plastic spatula. When the puree is finished, it is ready to toss with hot, freshly cooked pasta. If you wish to freeze all or part of the pesto, spoon into a freezer container. To prevent freezer burn and discoloration spoon a thin layer of oil over the pesto. Seal

and freeze. When you want to serve your basil pesto, thaw, warm gently, toss with your favorite pasta and enjoy!

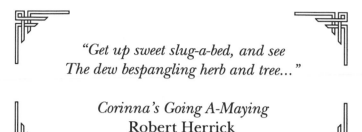

"Get up sweet slug-a-bed, and see
The dew bespangling herb and tree..."

Corinna's Going A-Maying
Robert Herrick

Herbed Butter and Cheese

Butter and cheese have a short refrigerator life. Use cheese within a week. Butter stays fresh two or three weeks. The flavor is enhanced by combining the ingredients the day before you plan to use or give. Because you are a busy herb lover, begin with the pre-softened, tub style butter or margarine before you go to softening, creaming, and shaping. There is no flavor like real butter; however good judgment should direct you to the product best suited to your dietary needs.

HERBED BUTTER
Materials:
　　4 ounces of butter (whipped or stick)
　　1 tablespoon fresh herb
OR
　　1 teaspoon dry herb
　　Container to store butter

Preparation:
　　In a mixing bowl, cream butter and add herbs. When using a stick of butter, let it come to room temperature before blending. Pack into small container, cover, and refrigerate until using or giving.
　　Hint: Herbed butter may be used on every occasion as you would use the unflavored. It is good tossed with pasta, on baked potatoes and other vegetables as well as hot breads. At a tea party or dinner with friends you could serve a variety of butters garnished with fresh herbs. Cut butter in pats or designs.
　　A gift which surprises and delights is a loaf of home baked bread accompanied by a container of herbed butter. Do not be overcome or discouraged, busy herb lover, by baking bread. Here is mix ahead,

sure to succeed and create "Ahs" recipe passed to me by a busy friend.

LOVINGLY LONG METHOD, HEATHER'S NO-FAIL BREAD
Ingredients:
    5 1/2 to 6 1/2 cups unbleached flour (first 3 can be whole wheat flour if you want to make whole wheat bread.)
    2 packages dry yeast
    2 tablespoons sugar
    1 tablespoon salt
    1/4 cup margarine
    2 1/4 cups very warm water (If the water is too hot it will kill the yeast.)

Preparation:
    In a very large bowl mix 2 cups flour, yeast, sugar, salt and margarine.
    Gradually add warm water to the dry ingredients.
    With the electric mixer blend on medium speed for 2 minutes.
    Add 1 cup flour and mix on high speed for 1 minute.
    With wooden or large cooking spoon gradually stir in the remaining flour one cup at a time until the dough is soft and moist but not sticky. (You might not need all the flour; begin watching carefully at 5 cups.)
    Flop dough onto floured board or counter top and knead for 8 - 10 minutes. (You don't know how to knead? Put dough in a mound. Press into the center with the heels of your hands and push away. Fold the dough in half toward you. Push again. This time fold the sides into the middle. Push again and repeat this over and over. The motion becomes self-hypnotic, rhythmic. You will see the texture change, and the dough will become smooth, elastic, with small air blisters.)
    After kneading, round the dough into a smooth mound, cover with plastic wrap and a clean dish towel, and let rest 10-15 minutes.
    Uncover and with your fist, punch down into the center of the dough.
    Divide the dough into 2 loaves.
    Place loaves, smooth side up in greased bread pans.
    Lightly brush the tops of the loaves with oil or margarine.
    Cover very loosely with plastic wrap, then cover with the dish towel.
    Refrigerate 2-24 hours.
    Before baking, remove loaves from refrigerator and let stand at room temperature for 10 minutes.
    Bake at 375 degrees for 30-35 minutes.The top will be golden, and

the bread will sound hollow when thumped.

BUSY HERB LOVER METHOD
Ingredients:
    One loaf of frozen bread dough from the nearest grocery store.

Preparation:
    Follow directions on the package.
    Thaw, let rise and bake.

HERBED CHEESES
    Evidently, the dairy industry is now sensitive to the "healthy eaters' dilemma" concerning calories, cholesterol, and fat. Not only are low fat and no fat cottage cheeses available, but also low fat and no fat cream cheeses are appearing in the supermarket dairy departments. Herbed cottage cheese can equal cream cheese when spread on a toasted bagel. Thinned carefully with a low or no fat mayonnaise or milk, the herbed cottage cheese can be used as a dip for vegetable strips or toasted pita bread wedges.

COTTAGE CHEESE
Ingredients:
    1 cup cottage cheese
    Selected herbs
    No fat mayonnaise

Preparation:
    Whirl cottage cheese at low speed in blender if your desire a smooth dip.
    In a small bowl combine cottage cheese and herbs.
    Add mayonnaise a teaspoon at a time until the desired consistency is achieved.
    Cover, refrigerate for at least 2 hours.

    Hint: Mix at least 6-8 hours before you plan to give or use. The flavors need time to blend or "marry" as my Great Aunt Emily used to say.

Suggested Combinations: (For eight ounces of cottage cheese)
    1 tablespoon minced spinach, 1 garlic clove minced, 1/4 teaspoon powdered sage (1 tablespoon finely minced if you have fresh sage.)
OR
    2 teaspoons dried commercial Italian herb blend, 1 teaspoon

chives, 1 clove of minced garlic (1/2 teaspoon garlic salt).
OR
    1 tablespoon fresh chopped basil (1 1/2 teaspoons dried), 1 teaspoon chopped parsley, 1-2 teaspoons grated onion.

HERBED CREAM CHEESE
Ingredients:
    8 ounces of cream cheese (in block or whipped in tub)
    Herbs of choice.

Preparation:
    Bring cream cheese to room temperature.
    In a medium bowl combine cream cheese and herbs.
    Pack the cheese into a crock or another attractive container unless you choose to roll the cheese into a ball or form a log.
    If you prepare a cheese ball, roll the ball in grated pecans, paprika, or a dry herb or herb combination which has been crushed with mortar and pestle.

    Hint: Eliminate the mixing. Shape the cream cheese into bite-size balls and roll in a dry herb mixture. Most blends work equally well for cottage cheese and cream cheese. Have fun with herbs and create blends to your taste.

    Suggested Combinations:
    1 teaspoon dried parsley, 1 teaspoon dried oregano, 1/4 teaspoon hot sauce, 1 tablespoon worcestershire sauce, 1 tablespoon minced, fresh onion, 1 clove garlic, minced. Roll in dried parsley.
OR
    1 tablespoon chives, 1 tablespoon mayonnaise, 1 teaspoon thyme, 1 teaspoon basil, 1 teaspoon marjoram.
PACKAGING FOR GIFT GIVING
    Basket of your choice.

"The lover of nature is he whose inward and outward senses are still truly adjusted to each other."

Nature
Ralph Waldo Emerson

According to the basket dimensions, with pinking shears cut an oversize square of fabric. (The pattern is your choice.) This might be too much for the busy herb lover, so substitute an attractive napkin or a colorful, new cotton bandana.

Drape the fabric in the basket; arrange bread (wrapped in clear plastic, tied with a bow) along with cheese or butter (in tub or on an attractive disposable plate) garnished with fresh herb or a sprig of fresh herb tied in with the bow.

OR

Recycle a disposable plastic or aluminum tray. Use an attractive placemat (the sixth one that never got used), paper placemat, or large lace paper doily. (No large doily?Overlap two, three, or four.)

OR

Use a giftwrap tote bag or spray paint a brown grocery bag.

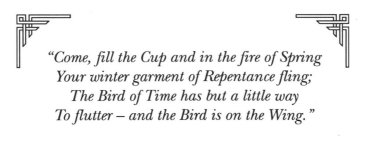

"Come, fill the Cup and in the fire of Spring
Your winter garment of Repentance fling;
The Bird of Time has but a little way
To flutter – and the Bird is on the Wing."

The Rubaiyat of Amar Khayyam of Naishapur
Edward Fitzgerald

Herb Jelly

Jelly from herbs? As a rule, herb jelly is not linked with peanut butter or considered at breakfast for toast and muffins. Rather, herb jellies lend a delicate flavor to luncheon biscuits or as delicious accompaniment for a variety of roasted meats. Traditionally, the herb jelly base is apple or grape juice. Most culinary herbs work well with these juices. Cinnamon and ginger are good companion spices. Have fun. Experiment!

LOVINGLY LONG HERB JELLY METHOD
Materials:
   8 ounce jelly glasses with 2 piece tops or paraffin to seal
   Large kettle

Ingredients:
   3 cups apple juice
   1/2 cup cold water
   3 to 3 1/2 cups granulated sugar
   1 tablespoon lemon juice
   2 tablespoons dried herb or 1/4 to 1/2 cup minced fresh herb
   1 box powdered fruit pectin
   Food coloring, if desired

Preparation:
   Scald and drain jelly glasses and lids.
   Heat together 1 cup apple juice and the herb.
   Bring to just under the boiling point.
   Remove from heat, steep for 30 minutes.
   Strain the herb mixture into your preserving kettle.
   Add remaining juice, water, lemon juice, food coloring, and pectin.
   Bring to a boil and immediately add sugar.
   Stir constantly, bringing mixture back to a boil.
   Boil for one minute.
   Pour into sterile jars, add a sprig of fresh herb if you wish, and seal either with the ring tops or paraffin.
   Yield: 5 eight ounce jelly glasses.

Hint: This jelly is rather pale. If you are not satisfied with the natural color, experiment! Green food coloring gives mint jelly a more appealing color. Red works well for apple cinnamon jelly.

Variations:

TRADITIONAL GRAPE BASE HERB JELLY
3 cups bottled grape juice
1/2 cup cold water
2 tablespoons cider vinegar
1 package powdered pectin
4 cups granulated sugar
1 teaspoon peppermint extract or 1/2 cup bruised mint leaves
Follow the jelly making directions already given. The only change
is to stir in the extract just before filling the jars.

More Variations: Apple with cinnamon stick, thyme or marjoram.
grape with tarragon. Try using cranberry juice for the base.

THYME FLAVORED GRAPE JELLY
1/3 cup finely crumbled thyme
2 cups bottled concord grape juice
1 lemon (use all the peel from the lemon)
3 tablespoons lemon juice (the juice of the peeled lemon)
3 cups of sugar
1/2 cup honey
1 box powdered fruit pectin
Sterile self-seal canning jars
In a large stainless steel or enamel sauce pan bring grape juice,
thyme and lemon peel to a boil. Remove from the heat, cover and let
steep for 20 minutes. Strain the liquid through a jelly bag or cheesecloth back into kettle or saucepan. Stir in sugar until it is completely
dissolved. Return to the heat and add honey and lemon juice. Bring
this mixture to a boil, add the powdered pectin and boil for just one
minute. Remove from heat and skim off any foam. Fill the hot sterile
jelly jars, put on the two piece top, tighten the ring and invert for 5
minutes. Put the jars in an upright position to cool. While the jelly
cools, make labels and put them on before you store the jelly. This will
save you confusion and provide a gift at a moment's notice for those
unexpected occasions.

TARRAGON FLAVORED WINE JELLY
1/3 cup finely crumbled dried tarragon leaves
3/4 cup lemon juice (fresh or concentrate)
2 generous strips of lemon zest, finely grated
1 1/2 cups dry white wine (Sauterne will do, however you will
meet with certain disaster if you use white wine vinegar or light cook-

ing sherry!)
    4 cups sugar
    1 box powdered fruit pectin or one half of a 6 ounce bottle liquid
pectin.
    Follow the directions for preparing Thyme Flavored Grape Jelly.

TROPICAL ROSEMARY JELLY
    6 tablespoons finely crumbled dried rosemary
    1 1/2 cups canned unsweetened pineapple juice
    1 orange (use both the juice and the rind)
    1/4 cup lemon juice
    3 cups sugar
    1 cup honey
    1 box powdered pectin
    Follow preparation instructions for Thyme Flavored Grape Jelly.

SPICY TOMATO BASIL JELLY
    1/2 cup finely crumbled dried basil leaves
    1 1/2 cups tomato juice (Why not try V-8 for a change?)
    1/2 cup lemon juice
    4 cups sugar
    1/2 to 1 teaspoon Tabasco sauce (suit your taste)
    1/2 6 ounce bottle liquid pectin
    Follow preparation instructions for Thyme Flavored Grape Jelly.

BUSY HERB LOVER'S METHOD
Materials:
    Double boiler
    Commercially prepared apple jelly
    Herb of choice
    Heat resistant, fancy glass dish or mold

Preparation:
    Place "store bought" apple jelly in double boiler and melt.
    As the jelly melts over this indirect heat, add herb or spice
    Stir gently as you heat the ingredients for 15-20 minutes.
    Strain, return to its jar, or pour into a lightly oiled, fancy mold to
chill. The jelly will reset. This must be refrigerated to stay fresh.

"Sweet spring, full of sweet days and roses..."

Virtue, George Herbert

Crystallizing Herbs

This is one of the mysterious realms that easily intimidates the busy herb lover. As a child, I believed that these curious delights, especially crystallized violets nestled in delicate crystal dishes, were found only in my Great Aunt Emily's Victorian brownstone home in New York City. It was not until money was dear, I was an at-home mother with four small children, and was trying to dress up a small roasted chicken that I discovered the simplicity of the process. Children are welcome help with this activity. If you have no children, borrow a neighbor's child. It's interesting and refreshing to see things from a child's perspective now and then. Grapes are ideal for the small fingers and the inexperienced. Do not be afraid of leaves or blossoms. They are not as delicate as you might suspect. My theory is that if it is edible, try crystallizing it.

Materials:
    Small watercolor brush
    Waxed paper
    Large shallow pan
Ingredients:
    1 egg white beaten until frothy but not stiff
    1/2 cup superfine granulated sugar
    Petals, leaves or whole flowers

Preparation:
 Collect, wash, and gently pat dry the herb to be used
 Paint egg white on each side of the leaf or flower
 Sprinkle the superfine granulated sugar so that all areas of the leaf or blossom are covered. (Do this over your sugar bowl that is on waxed paper so you don't loose sugar.)
 Gently place leaf on waxed paper lined pan and set in a warm, dry place for 2 - 3 days. If you use the refrigerator method to dry, it will take up to a week.
 Store in an airtight container. Use waxed paper to separate layers.

 Hint: Mint leaves and violets are traditional favorites. Try sage, rose petals, or geranium leaves. Use these as a garnish for cookies, cakes, and other deserts. Don't overlook dressing up fruit salads, meats or buffet platters. Offer crystallized mint as an after dinner palate refresher.
 Suggestion: To enhance the color of the flower, petal, or leaf try coloring the superfine granulated sugar. This is a judgment call for proportions. In a jar pour 1/4 cup of sugar, add one drop of food coloring, close up jar and shake to mix. Add more sugar or coloring until you are satisfied. In an airtight container store the remaining sugar to use for cakes or cookies.

Herbal Teas

 Advertising agencies, novelists, and British citizens would have us believe that "taking tea" is the civilized thing to do. Historians suggest that tea drinking was recommended by the wise Confucius of China. He realized a need to purify the drinking water. He promoted tea drinking because boiling water to make tea was a simple way to achieve the purification process.
 Sometime in Seventeenth Century England taking tea became a social pastime for the wealthy. The tea party in the American colonies was so important that the ladies switched to blending herbs for "Liberty Teas" when the Revolution was upon them and black tea was no longer available in the colonies after The Boston Tea Party.

My first recollection of having "Teapot Tea" was as a small child on a large chair in the presence of Great-Aunt Emily. Most of her teas were black tea enhanced with a "pinch of something," as she called it, from one of the mysterious jars in her glass door kitchen cupboard. Depending upon the occasion, sometimes the weather or to celebrate the change of seasons or the new moon she pinched apple mint, rose geranium or lemon balm into the pot. On occasion if "we" were coughing she added a dash of sage or rosemary. As I grow in kitchen experience, I think I am close to breaking the pinch and dash measure code. I'll never know for sure.

I have an elderly neighbor who loves to invite guests to herb tea tasting sessions. She recalls at one particular tea party early in her hostessing serving several varieties of tea. She uses certain cups for certain teas. To her surprise some of her guests traded cups and overindulged on the tasty herbal teas. Her plan for a lively afternoon was shelved as the guests rapidly reached a state of "relaxation" that neither she nor her guests expected. With the herbs offered here used in moderation, you should have no adverse effects.

INDIVIDUAL HERBS FOR TEA
Chamomile Flowers
Rosemary
Lemon Balm
Sage
Sweet Woodruff
Apple
Thyme
Orange
Peppermint
Wild Blackberry leaves
Spearmint
Wild Strawberry leaves
Rose hips
(Use dried not fresh wild berry leaves)

All these herbs may be brewed by infusion except lemon balm and rose hips. These should be prepared by decoction. Begin by brewing individual herbs, then add others one at a time to achieve the taste that pleases and refreshes you. No guilt feelings, busy herb lover, if you include black or orange pekoe tea in your blends. For a time, I suffered cultural confusion. My Kentucky grandmother had me believing I should drink plain herb tea for medicinal value, yet her New York sister, Great-Aunt Emily, suggested for serious social tea drinking

I must include black or orange pekoe tea in the blend. I grabbed whatever tea was sold in bulk on the grocery shelf. I doctored it with herbs until I found the proportions yielding flavors that satisfied me. These blends and suggestions are not the last word, but a gentle nudge to get you going.

BLENDS FOR THE BUSY HERB LOVER
MINT TEA
1 tablespoon crushed whole cloves
1 cup loose tea (black or blended)
1/2 cup dried mint leaves
2 tablespoons grated, dried orange peel
Mix together and store in an air tight container

LEMON GINGER TEA
Use the ingredients for Mint Tea, substituting grated, dried lemon peel for the orange peel and adding 1/4 teaspoon powdered ginger.

SPICED TEA
1/2 pound bulk orange pekoe tea
1/4 cup dried, grated orange peel
3 pieces of stick cinnamon (broken up but not pulverized)
4 tablespoons whole cloves
Mix together and store in an airtight container

HERB TEAS
Rosemary, lavender, whole clove, dried lemon peel
Rose hips and mint
Sage, apple mint, dried orange peel
Sage, thyme, rosemary

LEMON BALM TEA
(If you plant herbs, let this be one of the first. It is easy to grow, has myriad uses, and spreads rapidly.)
Fresh lemon balm (10 sprigs and whole cloves in 2 cups hot water simmered for 10 minutes)
4 whole cloves
2 tablespoons honey
1 tablespoon lemon juice

HEARTY LEMON BALM TEA
1/2 cup fresh peppermint leaves
1/3 cup lemon balm leaves

1 teaspoon rosemary
2 sage leaves

BREWING TEA BY INFUSION

Hopefully, busy herb lover, you own a teapot. If not, by all means invest in one. You can make tea in a pan on the stove; however, you

will find that there is something quite satisfying about pouring freshly brewed tea from a teapot. China, earthenware, or glass teapots are recommended for tea making. It could be my personal peculiarity, but metal seems to alter the flavor. At the elbow of my Great Aunt Emily, I learned to make tea. As a young bride I was put through a refresher course by my husband's Scottish grandmother before she presented me with my official "going to housekeeping" teapot. The secret revealed to me was this:

Preparation:

Fill a big pot or tea kettle with water.

Bring the water to a boil and fill the teapot with the hot water.

Let the teapot warm while you heat more water to the boiling point.

Pour out the water used to heat the teapot.

Spoon your tea or herb in a teaball or loose in the teapot, and carefully refill the pot with fresh hot water.

Cover the pot with a "cosy" or towel to keep it warm while the tea is steeping.

Keep the kettle warming on the stove so you can add hot water to dilute the tea if it becomes too strong.

Hint: A teaball, probably the forerunner of a teabag, is a small container immersed in the teapot that holds tea leaves so they aren't loose in the pot. It is easily available where kitchen gadgets are sold. Teaballs in fancy shapes can be ordered from many herb or gourmet catalogs. Some may believe that the full essence is not released unless the herbs free float.  If you choose this method, invest in a small tea strainer. Again, the tea strainers are readily available in any kitchen gadget department. Ornate silver strainers, wee double spoons that squeeze the leaves, and other curious sieve devices are available from catalogs.

Gift Packaging Suggestions:

The way to dress up a gift, in my opinion, is to present it in a handmade cloth bag. Items like herb vinegars are a visual treat and need no further adorning. A self-seal or twist-tie close bag of dry herbs tucked in a colorful cloth bag tied with ribbon hints of good things to come. Clearly, it is to your advantage to keep a supply of wrapping bags on hand for spur of the moment or almost forgotten occasions requiring a small gift. When I assemble the bags, I seldom rush right over to the fabric shop for materials. I look around the house to recycle remnants from other projects, my daughter's outgrown calico dress, muslin curtains lost in the hall closet. Once as I really got going into bag making, I could spot the scraps in 5x10 inch increments. Depending on the character of the fabric, ribbon, lace, shoe lace, yarn or twine make good bag ties.

LOVINGLY LONG BAG MAKING METHOD
Materials:
10"x10" fabric of your choice
15" ribbon, lace, twine, etc.

Preparation:
Cut the fabric to make two 5"x10" pieces.
Pin the right sides of the fabric together.
Machine stitch around three sides, leaving one 5" side open.
Turn bag right side out.
Evenly fold the opening fabric in around the top.
With a steam iron press the seams and the fold.
Tie the bag with ribbon of choice after filling it.
Hint: If you are making a quantity of bags and know the tie you want to use, simply cut it and store it in the bag until ready to use.

BUSY HERB LOVER'S METHOD
Materials:
10"x10" fabric
Fabric glue

Preparation:
Fold the fabric in half with the right sides inside, pinning corners together.
Following fabric glue directions, spread a fine line of glue across

the bottom to the open side.

Repeat gluing procedure working from the bottom corner to the top. (You will make an "L" with the glue.)

Let glue dry according to manufacturer's instructions.

Turn bag right side out and press with a warm iron.

Tie with fastener of your choice.

Suggestion: Be creative with the sizes as well as the fabric. I find that 12" x 18" makes an attractive larger bag. Try smaller bags for tiny remembrances. Busy Herb Lovers are thrifty. Experiment to come up with the size that best suits your needs and most of all, work with your fabric supply.

Gift Suggestions:

HERB TEA PARTY BASKET
Materials:
Herb Tea(s)
2 mugs
Gingersnaps or Gingerman (store bought or homemade)
Plastic sandwich size bags
Medium basket adorned with Spanish moss, dried herbs, flowers (Complete instructions found in craft chapter.)

Preparation:
Gently fill plastic bags 2/3 full with cookies.

Place cookie bags in mugs so the closure doesn't show.

Place mugs in basket.

Nestle the herb tea bags around the cups. (Hopefully, you were able to color coordinate the mugs with the print of the bags.)

Variation: Often for a wedding gift, I give an expanded version of the tea basket. I include a tea kettle and teaball. If there is room I add a small jar of honey and a honey server. There are times I use an unadorned basket and line it with an attractive linen towel or over-size linen napkin.

Chef Baskets

Materials:
Assorted sizes of baskets (with or without handles), rattan plates
Co-ordinated potholders and kitchen towels
Wooden kitchen utensils
Assorted kitchen gadgets appropriate to theme of gift

RICE LOVER'S BASKET
Preparation:
Use a kitchen towel or fabric with a cat motif to line an oval basket.
Fill two quart size zipper seal bags half full with Dill Rice.
Expel the excess air from bag and roll it.
Secure the roll with bright ribbon or yarn.
Fill two cloth bags, one with an eight ounce can of salmon, the other an eight ounce can of peas.

Variation: For a small gift, fill an airtight container with Tarragon Rice. Create a bag to fit the container. Make a gift card by gluing extra fabric to the back of a blank index card; fold the card in half when the glue is dry.

TACO TREAT BASKET
Preparation:
Spray paint a basket red.
Glue yellow ball fringe around the outer rim of a basket.
Glue a small artificial parrot or other multi-color bird to the handle.
Fill basket with a box of taco shells, chunk of cheddar cheese, several small bags of taco seasoning.
Include a cheese grater with red bow on the handle; for a larger basket, add packages of red, green or yellow paper plates and napkins.

SALAD BOWL
In a large salad bowl arrange a cruet of herbal vinegar and a cruet of light oil.
Include packets of herb blends.
Repackage into smaller zip close bags a variety of pasta as a base for pasta salad. (Use spinach and tomato pasta for colorful contrast.)

THE KITCHEN GOURMET
Preparation:

Glue one inch wide eyelet ruffle around the rim of a basket (any shape, any color).

Include a sampling of vinegars, salts (whatever has turned out to your liking).

Add wooden spoon, spatula, (whatever appeals to you and adds to the overall eye appeal of the basket); a mitt-style potholder and matching kitchen towel (consider for whom the gift is intended).

Add favorite recipes on cards or a small cookbook. (In every locality churches, service groups and civic organizations have cookbooks. Support your community by including one of these.)

Suggestion: Should the kitchen gourmet present be for a gentleman, eliminate the ruffle trim and line the basket with two plaid placemats, napkins, or other fabric. If you use colorful potholder and towel combinations, select a basic solid color for the lining.

Variation: Many of the teas, herb salts and blends can be done up in small bags and attached to wreaths. Refer to the craft section for ideas about adorning wreaths.

"She wrapped it up; and for its tomb chose
A garden-pot, wherein she laid it by,
And cover'd it with mould, and o'er it set
Sweet Basil, which her tears kept ever wet."

Isabella or The Pot of Basil
John Keats

Herbs for Comfort and Beauty

Was there ever a time when men and women didn't want to look good, smell good? In addition to lotions, rinses, creams and powders, women went so far as to put drops of belladonna in their eyes, enlarging the pupils, giving them a dreamy-eyed look. Have we changed? Mercy, no! We have come full circle to contact lenses that will let us change the color of our eyes. According to our own personal agendas, we still massage, anoint, soak, lather and in general pamper our bodies, fingernails, teeth and hair. Look at an hour of afternoon television, and you will see advertisements aimed at our personal vanities. There aren't enough hours in the day to wash, rinse, spray, gel, mousse or color with the number of products suggested for hair care. Some bath products take us away while others bring us back to life.

But woe to the bather who spends too long in the tub! Waterlogged prune skin. Check out the lotions and the powders.

Dear herb lover, we can spend big money on these products, or we can create our own lotions, astringents, rinses and other beauty care products with plenty of love and at minimal expense.

Once you know the ingredients for which to look, you will see them everywhere. The good old standby sources are the kitchen cupboard, the fresh produce section and seasonings shelf at the grocery store. Pull items from flower arrangements that come to you on special occasions. Check out the backyard. If yours is at all like mine, the tenacious wild things such as honeysuckle, violets, Queen Anne's lace, and assorted thorny, burr-spewing plants grow undaunted. Do not overlook vacant lots, meadows and patches of unruly things growing along rural roads for collecting. By all means ask permission to gather if the property isn't abandoned. Most people are happy to share what is theirs if you explain what you are doing.

This year for the first time I had to harvest bayberries from a neighbor's stand of bayberry bushes. Because of a major housing development nearby, my quiet rural neighborhood has become a suburban bedroom community. In this once bountiful area, I frown upon developers as they defoliate. Now I must compete with rabbits, raccoons and squirrels for nuts and berries. At least once and sometimes twice a day I walk with my faithful dog, Josie. I never set out for a walk without a bag and small scissors. Josie knows when I say "Hold it!" to stop and sniff because we'll be a while as I go about my gathering. In the days of small children, I had a similar bag tucked down in the stroller. My oldest son, now a man, still remembers dragging through the woods with me hunting and cutting the beautiful fan shaped fungus from rotting logs. My daughter recalls seeing me appear on a videotape poking and picking in the pine woods behind her intermediate school. The coach had videotaped their softball practice efforts.

Another option for obtaining herbs is by mail order. At the end of the book you will find a list of sources to order dried herbs and living plants.

Plan ahead with your ordering and collecting if you have big gift giving intentions. I discovered that inspiration and supply do not always go hand in hand. It is rare to find the shy violet after May, just as it is next to impossible to find acorns, hazelnuts, and assorted pine cones in the heat of July.

Again, in the guise of planning ahead, consider a small garden. If you live in an apartment or townhouse, dear herb lover, why not cultivate a window box or a planter? In a small space you can grow an amazing variety of herbs such as basil, oregano, marjoram and sage, as well as botanicals like dusty miller, pansies, scented geraniums and many other flowers that lend themselves to drying. If you have a fence where the wild things grow, consider the artemisias, Silver King and Sweet Annie. I have collected a list of commonly used and readily available aromatic herbs. This is a beginner's list. Many more exotic herbs are available should you want to explore the vast area of aromatics. Once again, experiment. Give each herb the "sniff test." You will either like the scent or loathe it. I caution you not to bombard your nose. There is no cleansing the nose like there is cleansing the palate after finishing a course in a multi-course meal or sampling fine wines. Select a grouping and sniff within the group. Monday, sniff citrus; Tuesday sniff floral and so on. Use good sense with the scents, and you will not create a disagreeable mixture. You will notice that many of the herbs and botanicals listed may also be used in potpourri blends. Because I believe that potpourri is the epitome of herbal and floral sensual and visual delight, I have deliberately deleted a discussion of potpourri from this section. It deserves a section unto itself.

For the sake of aromatic organization, I have listed the following items in "scent" families:

FLORAL SCENTS
Carnation
Gardenia
Hyacinth
Lavender
Lilac
Lily of the valley
Rose
Scented geraniums
Violet

OUTDOOR/FRESH AIR SCENTS
Bayberry
Chamomile
Marjoram
Pine needles
Rosemary
Sage
Southernwood
Sweet Woodruff
Thyme

CITRUS
Lemon balm
Lemon peel
Lemon thyme
Lemon verbena
Orange peel

SPICE SCENTS
Allspice
Basil
Bay
Caraway
Cardamom
Cinnamon
Cloves
Coriander
Ginger
Mint
Nutmeg
Pennyroyal
Star Anise
Vanilla

After considering the list of scents, hopefully you will realize that most of the items are readily available in dried form. If you go foraging in the window box, backyard, or field, you should keep a few things in mind. The optimum cutting time is late morning after the dew has evaporated and just before the sun reaches its peak. To wait until later in the day towards evening is to harvest flowers of waning beauty and leaves with less aroma because the sun's warmth saps the leaves' natural scent-producing oils and the flowers of their peak colors. Plan to cut only what you can use. My Grandmother's words of "waste not want not" should become your words. The final but very important foraging tip is never harvest what you have not identified.

The purists would have us gather and prepare one specimen at a time. Since time is dear to the busy herb lover, items are gathered as time and availability permit. When the items to dry are carefully collected, spread newspaper in a convenient location to sort what you have gathered. By this time you should have decided by which method you will dry your collection. Long ago every housewife had a stillroom. This was her room for drying and preserving herbs, therefore space was never a problem. She also kept in this room a treasured book, a "stillroom book," in which she recorded herbal information, recipes and remedies. Bunches of herbs were gathered and hung from rough hewn beams, racks or makeshift lines strung from rafter to rafter. What was important then and continues to be is a dry atmosphere with good air circulation, away from direct sunlight.

Methods for Drying Herbs

TRADITIONAL HANGING

When gathering, leave long stems. Wash the foliage to remove sand, grit or any pollutants from the air. Discard any withered or discolored leaves. Make bunches of 4 to 6 stems (small bunches dry quickly). Although it may be eye catching, do not mix varieties of herbs together. Dry them in separate bundles. Label each bundle. Use 36-inch string or yarn to tie each bunch. This leaves a generous amount to tie when hanging. A clothes rack set up in an extra bedroom is a good drying arrangement. One of my friends uses a quilting frame as a makeshift hanging rack. Perhaps you have a garage, as I do, that you can use. My garage is dusty so I hang my herb bundles in paper lunchbags dotted with small holes. At times when hanging space in the garage is limited, I hang two or three bagged bundles from wire coathangers, then hang the coat hanger from a nail. The paper lunch bag method serves me well in two ways. First, the herbs stay dust free

and out of direct light. Although the paper
bag drying process may be slightly slower,
there is a second plus to this method. All I
have to do to remove the dry leaves from the
stems is to gently shake the bag, then work the
bag gently between the palms of my hands.
The leaves come away from the stems and
crumble in the bottom of the bag ready for
storage containers.

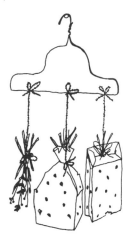

   Hint: Collect and keep all the bare stems.
They can be bundled and stored with the kin-
dling as scented fire starters. If you can't use
the stems, adorn them with ribbon and give as
a gift. Include directions for use.

TRADITIONAL AIR DRYING
This is a more challenging but equally effective method of drying. In
the simplest form you can use cheesecloth stretched tight between
bricks, cinder blocks, or sizeable books. An old screen makes an
acceptable drying rack, too. With a creative eye, look around to recycle
discarded wooden picture frames into drying frames. An ideal size is
12" x 18", but according to space, need and availability just about any
wooden frame will do. Simply staple cheesecloth or other open weave

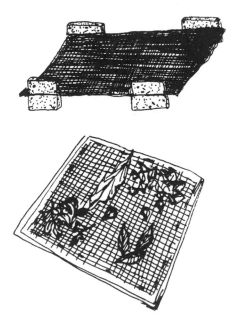

fabric to the edges of the frame. Give it the Marine Corps test: drop a quarter on the taut layer of fabric. If the coin bounces, the cloth is stretched to perfection. This is an air dry method, so wherever you put your drying frames, be sure to place them in a warm, well ventilated place away from direct sunlight. If you are really pressed for space, a frame elevated by books on two sides will do well under the bed. Once you have a drying screen prepared, the rest is simple.

To dry thick leaves such as basil or mint, remove leaves from the stems and spread in a single layer. Rose petals may be done the same way. Separate the petals from the flower head and spread in a single layer.

If you are handy with tools or know someone who is, you may want to consider making honest to goodness stackable drying trays.

HOW TO MAKE STACKABLE DRYING TRAYS

Materials:
   2" X 2" lumber (Length to equal approximately 7 feet. That will allow for one mistake cut.
   Fine screen wire nails (3 inch)
   Staple gun and staples or carpet tacks

Instructions for Making a 12" x 18" Drying Frame
   Cut two 12 inch lengths and two 18 inch lengths of wood. At each end nail the sections together to make a rectangular shape. The opening of the frame will be smaller than 12" x 18", so measure the interior rectangle and cut the screening one inch larger than the interior rectangle (both length and width). Stretch the screening across the frame, tack at each corner to hold. Staple or tack at half-inch intervals around the frame.

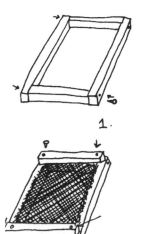

1.

2.

3.

4.

To make stacking trays, cut two more 12 inch pieces of wood. Nail the space bars to the short ends of the frame. Repeat this entire procedure to make other stacking trays. It is handy to have four trays. If you are ambitious, or housebound due to foul weather, you – or even better, the children – can sand the strips in preparation for you to stain and wax the wood. Nicely finished drying frames and an appropriate drying, preserving, botanicals book would make an unusual yet thoughtful gift for a gardener.

OVEN DRYING METHOD

This is a good method for the busy herb lover. It achieves the same results as air drying, but takes less time. You must be patient and vigilant while using this method because delicate leaves can darken, over-dry and loose their aroma as well as appearance. Set the oven on warm, no higher than 150 degrees. My first attempt at oven drying basil was a disaster. The oven was set at 200. The basil dried to a dirty brown-green and crumbled to powder. Not only did it loose its delightful aroma, but also it gave up its flavor. I use this method to dry orange, lemon, and grapefruit peel. (Surely you've bought a half bushel or so from the band boosters, a soccer team, or junior class at the local high school. What did you do with the rinds? Compost them? Good for you. More than likely those rinds got tossed in the garbage or put down the disposal, right?) Once again, I must remind you as I so often must do for myself. Stay focused on the project as you oven-dry these items. It is so easy to over-dry, draining the peel of its oils and turning it dark.

MICROWAVE DRYING METHOD

This is it, Busy Herb Lover, the all time speed method for drying! Once again, be careful not to over-dry. The instructions here are for a 600 watt microwave oven. The materials preparation is the same; however, drying time may vary according to the wattage of the microwave. Spread a quantity of washed leaves removed from the stems on a paper towel in a microwave-safe dish. Cover the leaves with an additional towel. One cup of basil leaves takes 2 to 2 1/2 minutes on high. Mint leaves are not as thick, so 1 cup of mint takes 1 1/2 to 2 minutes. You may be amazed at how moist the paper towel becomes. With this method, it is best to under- dry the herbs. Complete the process by air drying. Do put the herbs on dry paper towels to complete the process.

Hint: All the herbs you are saving for aromatic qualities store best in tightly covered glass jars away from direct sunlight. Check about every two days during the first week of storage. If any moisture appears on the cap or on the sides, you need to repeat the air drying process. If the moisture is allowed to remain, the herbs will mildew, and your harvest will be lost.

FREEZING METHOD

This is a simple, effective and efficient way of preserving herbs. Do not be tempted to try this method on herbs that need to retain their looks or be dried. Herbs for water, lotions and other suspensions are the exceptions. Freezing is most effective for culinary herbs. Consider what happens to a green pepper when it is frozen then thawed. Now visualize the perky mint leaf turning to thawed mush.

THE BUSY HERB LOVER METHOD
FOR DRYING HERBS AND FLOWERS:

Pick fresh herbs and flowers. Fill a mug or small vase with water. Arrange the cuttings in the container, enjoy, then overlook the cuttings when they pass their prime. When the cuttings feel papery dry, I take them from the container and cut off any moist part remaining on the stem and arrange them on a paper towel on a tray. This works well with arrangements from the florist that you just can't throw out. You don't have to part with those beauties. Roses dry well, carnations and statice too. If the petals don't dry to a satisfactory color, don't throw them away. Not all blends are meant for visual ecstasy.

"Where Corydon and Thyrsis met,
Are at their savory dinner set
Of herbs..."

L'Allegro
John Milton

Herbs for a More Beautiful You

Now that you have a small storehouse of dried herbs, treat your skin to simple herbal delights. It is known that women of wealth visit luxurious spas and pay dearly to refresh, revitalize and stimulate their skin. The good news, busy herb lover, is that you too can attain spa-like results by mixing a few herbs from the kitchen spice rack or your supply of home dried herbs to create facials, beauty baths, hair rinse, lotions and oils.

PREPARING AN HERBAL FACIAL TREATMENT
STEAM METHOD
This is an effective way to unclog pores and clean the skin. The preparation is similar to the old emergency remedy for breaking up chest congestion. Instead of clearing bronchial passages you will be pampering your skin.

Materials:
Low table
Comfortable chair
Large towel or beach towel
Basin or stainless steel stock pot
1 quart boiling water (use distilled water)
Herbs of choice (1 cup fresh or 1/4 cup dry)

Directions:

Place herbs in basin. Prepare an infusion by pouring boiling water over the herbs. Sit in the comfortable chair, put the towel over your head, bend over the steaming water and let the towel trap the steam. Relax and let the herbal steam work for about ten minutes. If you get too warm, lift the towel for a little fresh air. You won't undo the good. Rinse your face with fresh, lukewarm water. Although some people splash cold water or massage the face with ice after a steam facial, I prefer not to startle my pores closed with cold. I depend upon an herbal astringent.

Variation: You can create an herbal facial in the bathroom sink, but you will also discover your back gets tired bending over the sink. Part of the joy of herbal steaming is the relaxation factor. If you do select this method but hesitate to send the herbs down the drain or are reluctant fish them out of the sink, you can prepare a decoction by combining the herbs and water, bringing to a boil, and straining as you pour into the sink.

COMPRESS METHOD

This can be both a relaxing treat and at the same time beneficial. Frequently, when applied to the back of the neck, the compress will relieve tension headache. If applied to the cheeks and across the nose, the compress will open a clogged sinus while opening the pores. Set up as if you were preparing the steam facial. You will need to protect yourself from any dripping, so cover your chest and shoulders with an absorbent towel. Since the last thing you want to do is burn yourself, you must wait a few minutes before removing the washcloth from the prepared water. Use a spoon or tongs to lift the cloth. Squeeze slightly to remove excessive water. Your hands withstand heat better than your face, so if the cloth is too hot for your hands, you can be sure it is too hot for your face. Use your good judgment here, for your personal comfort.

Hint: Chamomile flowers are popular as an all-purpose facial cleanser. Do you want to encourage a youthful, natural healthy glow for your face? Consider lavender, peppermint, rosemary, and strawberry leaves to stimulate circulation. Yarrow works as an astringent to cleanse and close enlarged pores. Don't overlook rose petals to pamper your senses. These can be used individually or in any combination. The idea again is to experiment until you come up with a blend that satisfies you.

Herbs for the Bath

Is it showers for everyone these days? Does anyone take a "sit down" bath anymore? If the variety of bath accessories, additives and preparations is any indication, a goodly number of people must indulge. There are backrests, floating trays and waterproof radios for the serious bather. It is safe to say that bathing has continued to be a ritual of sorts from ancient times to the present. Even today, in some cultures bathing is a social, communal event performed for relaxation as well as cleansing. Historians tell us that public baths were popular in ancient Rome because only the very wealthy had baths in their homes. It is reported that every city had ornately decorated public baths. Through time, Rome remains renowned for the architecture of the public baths and breathtakingly beautiful statues that adorned the facilities. Some public baths included gardens and libraries. Historians note that the Baths of Caracalla in Rome had a capacity of 1,600 bathers and offered nearly two dozen varieties of bathing. Decisions, decisions! How did they keep from mixing up all those togas?

In the Middle Ages public bathing in England was forbidden when the baths became headquarters for prostitutes. That just about ended bathing in England for several centuries. The Puritans practiced cleanliness of the mind, but oh my, how they frowned on bathing. To them nakedness, even in preparation to bathe, encouraged sinful thoughts which led to sinful behavior. So much for personal hygiene. Is it any wonder that folks kept their noses in bunches of herbs? The good news is that about a century later Benjamin Franklin took time out from his kite and key experiments and his diplomatic missions to bring a bathtub back to his homeland from Europe. Since early American homes lacked proper "bath rooms," this tub in the shape of a lady's slipper was designed to hide the bather's body from prying eyes, thus ensuring privacy and keeping modesty in tact.

Today, we rush around working to pay the bills, struggling to meet the needs of others. Is it the "Puritan ethic" that tells us not to take time for ourselves, indulge ourselves in an aromatic, soothing, comforting, relaxing and yes, even at times invigorating herbal bath? If "cleanliness" is next to "godliness," as we are told, then let's by all means indulge in the personal luxury of herbal baths.

Herbal bathing in my house began with my daughter, Jenny. She was a motivated, record-setting, competitive swimmer for many years. Her dedication required being in chlorinated water several hours every day six days a week. Although she bathed to remove the chlorine, then lathered up with lotion, she still had itchy skin. Through trial and error we developed an herb and oatmeal mixture that soothed her skin. She was pretty disgusted seeing things floating around in the bath. Much to her delight, the same benefits of oatmeal and herbs could be derived when the mixture was enclosed in bags we made and floated in the water. The little bags made from porous fabric were refillable, too.

I have categorized the herbs in this section according to their action on the skin and to the psyche! You may wish to refer to the herbs listed by scent families. In making your herbal preparation, you can derive desired benefits to the skin as well as luxuriate with an appealing aroma. I am listing the most common, easy to find herbs as a starter list. There are others you may want to consider as your interest develops.

FRAGRANT HERBS
Bay
Clove
Scented geranium leaves (all varieties, however rose is a favorite)
Lavender flowers
Lemon peel
Mint (apple, pineapple, orange)
Orange peel
Rose petals
Rosemary

SOOTHING/RELAXING HERBS
Chamomile flowers
Lemon balm
Rose petals
Tansy flower heads
Violet (flowers and leaves)

STIMULATING/INVIGORATING HERBS
Basil
Bay
Lavender flowers
Lemon verbena
Marjoram
Mints (peppermint and spearmint)
Pine needles (fresh)
Rosemary
Sage
Winter savory
Thyme

HERBAL BATH PREPARATION

Select the water temperature that feels satisfying to you. Some beauty experts maintain that a warm bath will make you feel drowsy, a lukewarm bath will relax you, and a cool bath will invigorate you. Match your water temperature and the herbal variety according to your motivation (or lack of!). There is the universal caution to avoid extremely hot baths. You can become dehydrated, according to health experts, if the temperature exceeds 104 degrees. Exhaustion sets in, blood pressure drops, and you could faint. With six people in my house, I've never had to worry about too much hot water. I'm ever hopeful just to get a lukewarm, relaxing bath by the time it is my turn.

Infusing herbs, straining and adding to the bath water is a non-messy yet aromatic method to scent your bath. You can also make a simple herb bag by cutting a 6" round, double layer of cheese cloth. Fill it with 2-3 tablespoons of bath herb mixture. Gather up the circle, tie with a long string. Loop the string around the tub faucet (or showerhead for those of you who won't slow down long enough to take a tub bath) and let the water run through the packet as the tub fills. Float the little bag in the water during the bath. When you have completed your bath, toss the bag away, or open, discard herbs and rinse for the next time. Should you prefer to use an herbal bath bag as a washcloth, simply increase the dimensions by using an entire dishcloth or similar size muslin or multi-layered cheesecloth.

HERBAL BATH BAGS

Materials:

1 loose weave kitchen dishwashing cloth (makes 2 6" x 6" bags. For best results, do not use a tight weave dish drying towel.)

2 white dress shoelaces (18 or 21 inches) Twine works, but ribbon is a disaster. It bleeds and gets pretty disgusting looking when the water hits it.

Directions:

Cut dish cloth in half, for two bags.

Fold each half. Stitch up two sides, leaving one side open to insert the tie and a side with a factory hemmed edge for the top.

When stitching the third side, insert the folded shoelace two inches down from the top on the inside between the two

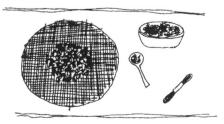

layers. The fold should peek between the edges of the fabric.

Stitch and turn the bag so what was the inside becomes the out-side, and the rough edges don't show. You will see that the bag has a long, handy tie for opening, closing, filling, refilling.

BATH BLENDS

LIFT YOUR SPIRITS BLEND:

Equal parts lavender flowers, apple mint leaves, crushed bay leaves, rosemary crumbled, and thyme.

Variation 1: Equal parts rose petals, rose geranium leaves, and mint (any variety).

Variation 2: Equal parts rose petals, lavender flowers, two tea-spoons orange peel (pulverized), two bay leaves (crushed), one tea-spoon each oregano and rosemary.

Variation 3: One cup rose petals, one half cup lavender, one half cup rosemary, one half cup lemon verbena, two teaspoons each thyme, marjoram and mint.

Hint: To pamper your skin while you lift your spirits, add an equal portion of old fashioned rolled oats to either blend.

ENERGIZING BLEND:

Lemon verbena, peppermint, rosemary, cinnamon geranium, cloves (crushed in mortar with pestle.)

Variation 1: Strawberry leaves, peppermint, lavender, and lemon rind (pulverized).

Variation 2 : Basil, bay, sage, thyme, and pine needles (snipped into one half inch pieces or smaller.)

CALM DOWN BLEND:

Chamomile flowers, violet leaves, lemon balm, and tansy button flowerheads.

Variation: Rose petals, strawberry leaves, lemon balm, four bay leaves (crushed).

"Indeed sir, she was the sweet-marjoram of the sallet, or, rather the herb of grace."

All's Well That Ends Well, Act IV, Scene V
William Shakespeare

Herbs for Skin Care

It's your skin, and you want to look good as well as smell good. Herbs are gentle to the complexion. By using herbal lotions you can rid your skin of excess oil. On the other hand, you can moisturize dry skin by adjusting the ingredients. There are two main types of herbal lotions, water based and alcohol based.

WATER BASED HERBAL AFTER BATH SPLASH:
Make herb water by gently bruising one cup leaves or flowers. In a stainless steel pan, gently heat the leaves or flowers in two cups of distilled water. Let the herbs infuse until the mixture is cool. Strain the mixture into a glass jar with a tight fitting lid or strain the mixture into smaller fancy bottles which you have recycled. This herb water is best used within one month.

The following herbs and flowers are known to possess astringent qualities and work well in herbal "after bath splash":

FOR OILY COMPLEXION:
Lavender
Sage
Yarrow
Pansy
Rose
Violet

FOR DRY COMPLEXION:
Chamomile
Clover
Parsley

To prepare a simple moisturizing lotion add two parts herb water to one part glycerine.

ALCOHOL BASED HERBAL AFTER BATH SPLASH:
Unlike its water based lotion cousin this herb preparation does not need to be refrigerated. It retains its potency at room temperature for several months. Following this method, you will be creating a strong preparation that will be diluted with distilled water, in a proportion of 1/3 alcohol-herb base to 2/3 water. Do not use heat this time. Heat will cause the alcohol to evaporate, therefore, eliminating the preservative power plus destroying the extra "tingle" effect.
Materials:
6 tablespoons of vodka or witch hazel. (Because of the strong medicinal odor, do not use rubbing alcohol.)
1 ounce dried herbs or flower petals. (Consult the scent families listed earlier in this section when selecting a desired aroma.)
12 tablespoons distilled water
Glass jar or small crock

Preparation:
Put the herb or herbs of choice into the jar. Gently spoon the vodka or witch hazel over the herbs. Cover with loose fitting top (plastic wrap etc.) and set aside for ten days. Strain through double thickness of cheese cloth, soft muslin, or try a coffee filter. Add the distilled water, shake to mix, then bottle.
Variation 1: Use crushed star anise for a manly, light licorice scent.
Variation 2: For a Victorian splash use lavender blossoms.
Variation 3: Try lemon balm and crushed cinnamon stick.

Hint: Do not be tempted to try powdered herbs and spices. The appearance of the splash will be less than appealing.

THE BUSY HERB LOVER METHOD:
Mix an essential oil with the distilled water and spirits in a glass container. Shake the mixture. You have a "splash" in an instant. Essential oils come in spice as well as herbal and floral scents. Once again, experiment!

LAVENDER SPLASH:
3 cups distilled water
6 tablespoons Vodka or witch hazel
12 drops lavender essential oil

Other Herbal Beauty Products

HERBAL OILS
Are you into oil massages? Create an herbal oil from your favorite scent.

Materials:
2 cups virgin olive oil, or canola oil
1 cup mixed fresh herbs
1/4 ounce essential oil

Preparation:
Mix the herbs and oil. Store in a glass jar for seven to ten days. Strain the blended herbs and oil through double thick cheesecloth. Add the essential oil and bottle.
Hint: If you want a speedy method or do not have herbs of choice available, use the same amount of oil, eliminate the fresh herbs, and

double the amount of essential oil. Shake and let sit overnight to produce a mellow scent.

AFTER BATH DUSTING POWDER
Materials:
   10 dry rose geranium leaves
   1/4 cup lavender
   1 cup unscented talcum powder
   Blender
   Jar to store scented powder

Directions:
   Combine rose geranium leaves and lavender in the blender
   Whirl the herbs until they are almost to a powder state
   Add the talcum powder and whirl again
   Store the powder in the jar and repackage in a more ornate box, basket or jar when it is to be given as a gift

THE BUSY HERB LOVER'S HERBAL SHAMPOO
For best results begin with a commercial baby shampoo and add an essential herb or spice oil for an appealing scent. To highlight your hair add a strong infusion of one of the following:
   Blond Hair: Chamomile. Turmeric
   Brunette or Black Hair: Rosemary, Clove, Mint, Yarrow
   Red Hair: Pot Marigolds, Hibiscus flower, Clove

Hint: For dry hair problems try adding fresh orange or lemon peel to the mild shampoo. Hair can become less oily with the addition of peppermint or wild blackberry leaves instead of citrus peel.

PET COSMETICS
Yes, busy herb lover, you read correctly! Pet cosmetics. Have you spent time bathing the dog only to see your best friend dart outside and roll in compost, underbrush or other earthy spots harboring fleas and strange unidentifiable odors? My blond Labrador retriever cons me each bath time because she is quite happy to hop into the bathtub. She's a water dog, it's in her nature, you say. No, she's neurotic, frightened to enter a body of water larger than a drainage ditch. In addition to her "aqua-phobia" she has bug paranoia. She snaps at insects, real and imaginary. A veterinarian prescribed medicated shampoo which helped rid her of the fleas. Not even a cedar shavings mattress would deter them from returning. Finally, after the thousandth mud roll, I realized she didn't like the way she smelled after a bath. She wasn't try-

ing to achieve a smell. She was trying to rid herself of "man-made odor."

I turned to my herbs, as I do in times of crisis, and started snipping. I have no idea what herbs I used in the first batch of dog rinse. I put everything in the largest kettle I owned, filled it with water, brought it to a boil, reduced to a simmer for half an hour. I covered it and let it sit on the back of the stove for the remainder of the day. That evening I strained the decoction and used it as a rinse. If a dog smiles, she did. I towel dried her, and she lounged on her doggie mattress. There was none of this frantic need to get outside and roll. The added bonus was a flea free dog for several days. To be realistic, the effects of the herbal rinse won't last forever. Three to four days is about the best you can expect. I have refined Josie's rinse and what follows seems to work for her. Again, as in all things, feel free to experiment and develop a rinse that can be made from herbs easily accessible to you and please your dog.

JOSIE'S RINSE
> 1 cup lemon balm (fresh stems and leaves)
> 1/4 cup lavender (fresh stems and leaves)
> 1/4 cup oregano (fresh stems and leaves)

Variation:
> 1 cup marigolds (fresh stems, leaves, and flowers)
> 1/4 cup peppermint (fresh stems and leaves)
> 1/4 cup rosemary (fresh stems and leaves)

Hint: No matter what blend you choose, include mint of some type in the mix. Mint seems to please the dog. If you substitute dry herbs for fresh, cut the ingredients by one half. Follow the directions for the simmering and steeping process.

MOTH AND INSECT REPELLENT FOR YOUR HOME

It is a sad but true fact of life, busy herb lover, if your indoor/outdoor dog or cat has a problem with fleas, you can be sure eventually your rugs and upholstered furniture will harbor the little biters too. It is quite an experience to return to the homeplace after a long vacation. The fleas are waiting for the first hairy leg. Grocery stores, hardware stores, lawn and garden places all have a variety of flea bombs and sprays. The yellow pages offer many exterminators. All of them seem to offer a chemical solution to the problem. The consumer receives constant reassurance that these products are non-toxic to us or our pets. Perhaps in the most extreme situations one could resort to chemicals. Inadvertently, we come in contact with so many chemicals that it is good to avoid exposure whenever possible. Our forefathers had fleas, body lice and other indelicate insect-induced conditions. The resourceful colonial housewife prepared herb combinations to combat household infestations.

FLEA REPELLANT

Catnip, peppermint, spearmint, tansy and rue seem to work keeping the fleas under control in my house. I tie small bunches of southernwood (when it is available) mint, tansy, rue and lavender and place them under couch cushions, beneath beds, chairs and dressers.

Hint: Daily vacuuming during the warm months helps too. Before you vacuum, crumble some dried mint and tansy leaves on the carpets. As you vacuum over the herbs, you will be freshening the air and also taking herbs into the vacuum bag. Remember, what goes in could be flea eggs ready to hatch in the bag. Disgusting thought, I know, but none the less true. If there is something in the disposable bag that will arrest the flea population that may develop you are that much further in the flea battle.

MOTH DESTROYER/REPELLANT

Throughout American history that old moth magnet wool was a mainstay fabric in most wardrobes. I am certain that the frugal colonial housewife had many moth destroyer recipes. A traditional colonial moth repellant was equal portions of tobacco and pot marigold leaves. If you choose not to smell like tobacco or cedar, try one of the following mixtures. Combine the dry herbs and spices, then store in a sealed container for about a week. Stuff little bags with your blends and tuck in chair and couch cushions, tie on coat hangers in closets, place in dresser drawers with sweaters, woolen gloves and scarves.

SPICY MOTH DESTROYER

1/2 cup thyme (crumbled)
1/2 cup tansy (crumbled)
1 cup lavender flowers
1 cup rosemary leaves
1 tablespoon allspice (powdered)
1 tablespoon cloves (crushed)
1 tablespoon lemon peel (crushed)
2 cinnamon sticks broken into tiny pieces

VICTORIAN ROMANCE MOTH DESTROYER

2/3 cup rose geranium leaves (crumbled)
2/3 cup lemon balm

2/3 cup lavender flowers
1/3 cup lemon verbena
1/3 cup rosemary
1/3 cup thyme

SIMPLE GIFTS FOR BEAUTY AND PLEASURE

Do you shudder, busy herb lover, when you get enthused about something, then read in the fine print that some "assembly" is required? Once again, making something for yourself is one thing; preparing it for gift giving is another: "assembly" is required. That's where so many of us end our ideas of the homemade, handmade gift. You say you don't have "clever" ideas? What is clever anyway? Think a while about the person who will receive your gift. Consider that person's likes. Are you arguing with me yet, trying to say you don't know what the individual likes? Usually a person is vocal about dislikes. Avoid the areas you know are negatives.

Gift giving can be a mine field. But it has been my experience that in giving or receiving a one-of-a-kind herbal "something" prepared for the specific occasion, materialism pales. Surprise is generated along with a genuine appreciation for the thought that went into the gift as much as the gift itself. I caution you, there is a yoke of responsibility that goes with the home-assembled gifts. Folks will begin to look forward to the next occasion, more herbal surprises. You can do it!

BATH BASKET
Materials:
Small basket
2 colored or decorated wash cloths
4 bath bags
2 varieties of bath herb (approximately 1 cup of each in see-through freezer bags, sealed and labeled.)

Directions:
Arrange washcloths in the bottom of the basket.
Tie the bath bags in a stack with ribbon that matches your color theme.
Tie the bath herb bags with the same or harmonizing ribbon.
Nestle the little packages in the folds of the washcloth.
Cover the basket with colored plastic wrap and secure the plastic on the bottom with cellophane tape.
Hint: Plaid or floral ribbon perks up the basket when the wash-

cloths are a solid color. This little gift ships well because the contents are secured with the plastic wrap.

Variation: This can be a token gift or enlarged to include towel, washcloth and loofa sponge. The loofa sponges are actually a form of squash. When the squash is peeled and carefully dried, it is a creamy beige neutral color and looks like a fibrous sponge. Loofa sponges are prepared for sale in various sizes and forms such as part of a bath mitt, as a hand held sponge, and with a handle to use as a back brush. Recipients are intrigued by the looks and the gentle comforting scrubbing capabilities of the loofa.

QUEEN FOR A DAY BEAUTY BASKET
Materials:

Large attractive willow or vine basket with handle (adorned with artificial ivy and silk flowers)

Assorted herbal beauty products

Bath herb packets

Bath bags

Lavender after bath splash

Scented talcum powder in an attractive container

Towel to which you have sewn a ruffle border

Washcloth to match towel

Extra wide terry head band

Inflatable, waterproof neck pillow

Bottle of sparkling spring water

Book of light verse

FACE THE MUSIC BEAUTY BASKET
Materials:

Small basket with handle

Half inch wide ribbon

Glue

Herb selections for facial sauna

Directions for preparation of the herbal sauna:

A timer or a miniature hour glass (There are a variety of sizes of timers. Some are automatic and go off with a startling ding or ringing. There are three, five, ten and twenty-minute "egg timer" style hour glasses available in kitchenware shops and catalogs.)

Extra wide stretchy headband

Cassette tape of classical mood music

Mendelssohn's music from "A Midsummer-Night's Dream"
Respighi's "Fountains of Rome"
Copland's "Appalachian Spring"
Six individually wrapped peppermint candies
White polyester fluffy filling, white excelsior, or other light colored packing material
Lacy fabric (enough to cover packing material)

Directions:
Make a four-loop bow with streamers.
Glue (with white glue or hot glue) bow to the handle.
Let the streamers dangle from the handle.
Spread a generous layer of fiber filling in the basket.
Cover the fiber filling with the lacy fabric.
Nestle the sauna herbs, directions, headband and cassette on the lacy fabric which covers the fiber filling.
Tie the packet of herbs and cassette tape with the ribbon used to decorate the handle.

BEAUTY IN A BASKET
Materials:
Small oval basket
Eyelet ruffle
Glue (white glue will do for this small project)
After bath herb splash
Small packets of individual herbs
Two or more small fabric sacks filled with cotton balls
Recipe to make more after bath herbal splash
Colored tissue paper

Directions:
Measure around the top of the basket, cutting enough eyelet to overlap one half an inch. (It is much better to have a little extra to trim off than come up short and have to piece in the gap with bits of ruffle.)
Glue the ruffle around the basket just under the rim.
Gently crumple tissue paper to make nesting material.
Place the after bath herbal splash at one end of the basket.
Arrange the sacks of cotton balls and bags of herbs in a way that is pleasing to your eye.
Tuck the recipe which you have printed on an index card or pretty stationary somewhere among the packets.
For shipping you may cover the basket with clear plastic wrap.

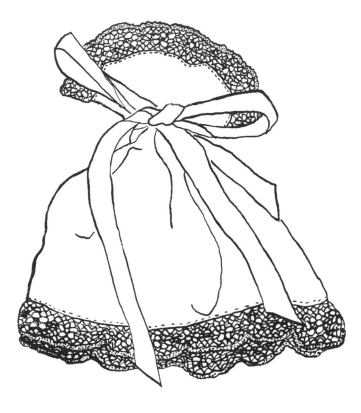

Sense Pleasing Scents

You know by now that through history, people have used herbs for air purification, medicinal properties and religious ceremonies. There are some however, who used herbs for personal arousal and seduction. What was Cleopatra's charm? Do you suppose her mattress – which historians say was stuffed with rose petals – was her subtle persuader?

In Medieval times the blushing young bride placed a bowl of fragrant herbs on a table near the bed in the wedding chamber. The bride offered lemon verbena, marjoram, a variety of mints, thyme, violets and other herbs known to be favored by Venus, the Goddess of Love. Basil was included to appease mighty Mars, God of War. These offerings were to bring abiding love in a strong argument-free marriage. Tradition has it that these special wedding night herbs were to be stirred occasionally with the fourth finger of the left hand. The forefinger on the right hand, which would be a logical stir finger, was never to be used to mix the wedding night herbs. In ancient times everyone knew that witches preferred to use the right hand to work their charms. The forefinger on the right hand was used by witches to point at their victims when cursing or casting spells upon them.

Christianity dispelled the pagan ideas and beliefs that surrounded herbs. Monks controlled the production of herbs. Although most large herb gardens were within monastery walls, herbs remained integral in daily life through the centuries.

It was not until the Nineteenth Century that herb use moved from medicinal to decorative. Because Queen Victoria, straight-laced and severe in most aspects of personal liberties, enjoyed scented floral and herbal blends, the English housewife felt free to enjoy this "sensual" pleasure. In considering the Victorian period and the names that were in vogue, you will see the elevated stature of flowers and herbs. Ivy, Flora, Rosemary, Iris, and Rose enjoyed popularity. My own Kentucky-raised Victorian era great-grandmother was Daisy. Is it possible that Victorian women who were obedient and outwardly subservient gained a secret identity which was nourished as they mingled with their herbs and flowers?

A number of Victorian writers likened women to flowers. Making dried and artificial bouquets and perfuming her household with her own personal recipes for scented floral and herb blends was a challenge for the Victorian woman. In the living room and drawing room after daily tidying up, the housewife opened her jar of rose buds or blended herbs and stirred them. This she did to freshen the air, indeed, the grand finale to her cleaning. Just as the stillroom book was important to the colonial housewife, the Victorian woman kept her herbal medicinal information and the recipes for her personally created scented blends in a private journal in her stillroom. She guarded this book of herbal blends as if she had charge of the royal treasure.

The purists began to recognize scents and in time identify the creator. I know that such a thing is possible. My own dear grandmother smelled of violets. I sat on her lap so many afternoons and smelled that violet scent as she read to me. To this day if I smell violets in a grocery checkout line, or as I pass the cosmetic counter in an upscale department store, I turn around fully expecting to see my grandmother.

The beautiful and fragrant blends of long ago that seem to be ever popular are known as potpourri. While the difficult to pronounce word might summon up exotic and strange thoughts, actually it is neither glamorous or mysterious when the name is examined. The

French words for "pot" and "rotted" combined give us the word, "pot-pourri". The roots of the word conjure a less than lovely thought; however pot and rotted are right on target and appropriately describe the process for making moist potpourri.

The earliest traces of "pot rotted" preparations are from Egyptian records. When an Egyptian king was buried, a container of fresh rose petals was placed with him in the tomb. As the petals rotted, a sweet scented aroma was released into the tomb. This scent was to provide fragrance for the king in his after-life.

Today, there are two kinds of potpourri, moist and dry. The moist potpourri has a strong long lasting scent, but it is pretty disgusting to look at. Don't let the appearance stop you from preparing this. The solution is to keep it out of sight. Whatever nontransparent container or crock you decide to use should have a lid. When you want aromatic pleasure, remove the lid and stir the contents. When your guests leave, or the room is sufficiently fragrant, replace the lid. With care, the moist potpourri will stay aromatic for nearly a year.

Dry potpourri is a visual as well as sensual delight. For this reason it is more popular than the moist. The major drawback is that the scent rapidly disappears and that ambrosial ecstasy you felt as the fragrance wafted from the lovely open dish is soon gone. Fortunately, there are preparations you can purchase to "refreshen" your potpourri. It is rather discouraging to me to see potpourri so commercialized. The romance quickly departs when I see the bags of magenta tinted strawberry scented wood chips masquerading in grocery and discount stores. At holiday time the wood chips take on bright green and red hues in the name of forest or holly. Be honest, busy herb lover, you have seen these bags, maybe you have bought them in your desire for "something special" in the air.

Preparing potpourri is fun and relatively inexpensive. It can be time consuming or not depending on the amount of effort you want to put into gathering, drying or purchasing the individual herbs and flowers. Do plan for a month to six weeks to set aside your blend so its fragrances blend properly. To rework a Victorian culinary term, you must let the aromas "marry". I have cataloged a list of mail sources for herbs and herbal needs. You will find this at the end of the book. Coming up with a personal blend is creatively satisfying. Enjoy the trip along the blending path. Experiment! Take my hand, and I will lead you down the garden path to potpourri.

You are a busy herb lover, so I will introduce you to some short-cuts. My methods are shortcuts. As I have told you, I am not a purist, I am an enthusiast. There are paths you can take to higher levels if you choose. But for now, be of good cheer, I will not leave you stranded as you begin preparation. Look to the bath herbs section and you will find the most easily obtainable herbs listed according to "scent families". This is by no means the "list of all lists," rather a nudge to get you started. You will want to add to the list, I am sure. As you increase your herbal knowledge, you will, with surprisingly little effort, increase your potpourri vocabulary. The mysterious language will be yours. The following are words of which you need working knowledge:

ESSENTIAL OIL (sometimes called fragrant oil):
This is a vital ingredient in dry potpourri. It is also used to freshen old mixtures. This oil is derived from the herb, flower, or spice. Essential oil, used alone or in combination with other oils, is what gives the blend its distinctive aromatic character. The fragrance from the essential oil will blend with the other ingredients, but it will still be the dominant scent. You wouldn't add violet oil to a blend that was supposed to have a citrus smell. The violet would dominate. However, if you wished to enhance a floral blend, violet would harmonize with other florals. The pure essential oils are rather expensive and can be purchased by catalog or from perfume suppliers usually located in metropolitan areas. Reasonably priced, very good synthetic oils are available at craft stores. The craft store essential or fragrant oils are often called refresher oils. Occasionally a well stocked pharmacy carries some of the oils. I have been able to get a potent oil of cinnamon and also oil of cloves from my local pharmacist.

It is an economy measure to extract your own essential oils. If you care to spend the time you will find this method easy and rewarding because you have done it yourself. In the top of a double boiler pour one cup of mineral oil. Slowly, carefully heat the oil so it is warm but not hot. Add to the oil two cups of fresh, fragrant flowers or herbs (individually or in an experimental blend). Try pine needles for a woodsy pine scent. Cover and let the flowers or herbs steep in the oil. Add 1 cup fresh flowers or herbs to the pot every thirty minutes. Try to keep the oil warm and at an even temperature. Each time you make an addition to the oil be sure to check on the supply of water in the bottom half of the double boiler.

You will know the oil and materials have blended when you lift the top and can smell a distinct fragrance. This will take two to three hours. Let the oil cool completely. With your fingers gently lift the material from the oil and gently squeeze to extract the remaining oil. Strain the oil as you pour it into a bottle. (Here is where a funnel is very useful.) You can use a decorative, recycled bottle but be certain that the bottle used for storing the oil has a tight fitting cap, cork or stopper.

FIXATIVE

This is the preparation you add to your herbs, flowers, and spices to literally "fix" the scent. Fixative is the mysterious ingredient that blends the fragrances into one special scent. It also ensures that the scent is powerful enough to remain for months because it prevents the natural oils of the herbs, flower petals and spices from evaporating. Fixatives are available in powder and crushed granules. Two types of fixative are animal and vegetable. Although the animal derivatives have fallen from grace in recent years as a result of sound ecological judgment and rising cost, they are more pungent and long-lasting than the vegetable fixatives. Fortunately, today there are synthetic animal fixatives available so if you see musk or ambergris you can be reasonably certain, unless marked otherwise, it is a synthetic preparation. When using a fixative, you should remember to use one tablespoon per quart of leaves and petals .

ANIMAL FIXATIVES

Ambergris: Source is the sperm whale. The scent is similar to balsam.

Civet: Source is the civet cat. The scent is a delicate floral.

Musk: Source is the male musk deer. The scent is strong and sweet.

VEGETABLE FIXATIVES:

Calamus: Source is the rhizome of sweet flag. The scent is light violet.

Orris Root (sometimes seen as orrisroot): Source is the rhizome of the Florentine iris. The scent is violet.

Resin (gum benzoin): Source is the bark of the spicebush. The scent is light spicy/floral.

Vetiver: Source is a tropical grass. The scent is similar to sandalwood.

UTENSILS NEEDED FOR PREPARING POTPOURRI:

Mortar and Pestle

Wooden Spoon: Metal must never be used.

Glass Mixing Bowl: Metal must never be used. Plastic and wooden bowls will absorb the fragrant oils, drawing the strength from this mixture and retaining the odor, spoiling any future use for the bowl.

Scoop: This tool for measuring is far superior to a spoon. The depth and size of the scoop is up to you. You will make less mess and have less waste using a scoop. A variety of plastic scoops are available in the kitchenware section of any discount store. If you prefer a fancy scoop, you can order from gourmet kitchen suppliers or herbal craft catalogs.

Eyedropper: Accurately measuring the essential oil is vital. An eyedropper is an efficient, economical measuring device. Eye droppers come in glass and plastic. They are usually available at pharmacies. If you choose glass, wash carefully after each use. You can use these for any of the oils. If you choose plastic, lay in a supply of eyedroppers. Since plastic absorbs, plan to use one dropper for each variety of essential oil. You don't have to be as particular about washing after use, if the plastic dropper is labeled and used for the same oil each time.

Scale: You can use the traditional kitchen "diet" scale for measuring herbs, flowers, and spices. Some recipes call for exact weights, some for pinches or handfuls. With each recipe follow the proportional directions exactly...the first time. Test the results when the mixture is prepared according to the recipe, then adjust according to your preference. Scales are necessary too when you create your own blends. Measure and record exactly the first time. If it turns out to your liking, you will know exactly what you did, and how you achieved it.

Potpourri

Moist Potpourri

LOVINGLY LONG METHOD
Materials:
   Wide mouth crock
   Plate to fit down in crock
   Paperweight or other heavy object to hold plate in place
   Wooden spoon

Ingredients:
   4 cups rose petals
   1 cup lavender flowers
   1 cup rosemary
   3/4 cup lemon balm
   1/3 cup lemon thyme
   1 teaspoon cinnamon (powdered)
   1 teaspoon cloves (powdered)
   1 teaspoon coriander (powdered)
   3/4 teaspoon nutmeg (powdered)
   1/2 teaspoon mace (powdered)
   1/2 cup orrisroot (powdered not pulverized)

Coarse non-iodized salt
Rose or lavender essential oil
Directions:
Spread the rose petals in a ventilated place or on a drying rack to dry for 24 hours.
Place one fourth of the petals in the bottom of the crock.
Cover with a light layer of salt.
Repeat the procedure until all the petals are used.
Put the plate down in the crock to pack the petals.
Place the weight on the plate to keep even pressure on the contents of the crock.
Store in a cool, dark place.
Add to the petal/salt mixture as more petals become available.
With each new layer, spread a layer of salt.
Let the contents age for two weeks after the last addition.
Check the crock every two to three days.
To remove excess liquid that might develop use the wooden spoon and discard the liquid.
During the third week combine all the other flowers, spices and fixative.
Using the wooden spoon gently blend the dry ingredients with the moist.
With eyedropper release five drops of essential oil onto the top of the blended flowers, herbs, spices and fixative.
With clean eyedropper release three drops of brandy onto the blend.
Cover tightly and let stand two to three weeks.
Repack into permanent container that has lid.
The blend is ready to use.
Remove top of container to reveal the fragrance.
Replace the cap when finished.
Hint 1: The older traditional varieties of roses have a stronger fragrance in their petals.
Hint 2: If you don't have essential oil on hand when your moist potpourri scent is no longer strong, you can use a few drops of brandy to refresh, replenish the fragrance.

BUSY HERB LOVER METHOD FOR MOIST POTPOURRI
Materials:
Refer to the list for traditional moist potpourri.

Ingredients:
4 cups rose petals (partially dried but not brittle)

2 cups assorted fresh flower heads (partially dry)
Violets
Lavender
Marigolds
Lilac
Any flower with a strong fragrance that appeals to you
1/2 to 2 cups aromatic leaves (select from the following or select
your own. Make sure the leaves are partially dry)
Rose or cinnamon geranium
Lemon balm
Lemon verbena
Mints (apple, orange, pineapple work well)
4 bay leaves (medium size, crumbled)
3 tablespoons allspice (powdered)
4 tablespoons cloves (powdered)
4 tablespoons brown sugar
1 tablespoon orrisroot (powder not granules)
2 tablespoons brandy
1 cup salt (coarse, non-iodized)

Directions:
Gently toss petals, flower heads, leaves with powdered orrisroot.
Combine spices, sugar and crumbled bay leaves with salt.
Pack 1/3 of the flowers and petals combination in a crock.
Cover with one-third of the salt-seasonings blend.
Repeat until you have three salted-down layers.
There should be a layer of salt on top.
On the salt carefully sprinkle the brandy.
Weight down the mixture and cover tightly.
Stir daily for five weeks.
Spoon into smaller containers with secure lids.
Hint 1: To give the moist potpourri your personal aromatic touch, replace the brandy with 2 tablespoons of your favorite alcohol-based perfume.
Hint 2: You can keep this mixture fragrant for many years by adding brandy or your perfume every six months.

DRY POTPOURRI
This is what you are used to. This is what you see bagged in the stores. This is the potpourri that is fashioned for its visual beauty as well as its aroma. Do you have a bag of inexpensive store-bought potpourri on hand? Look at it. Do you see the dreaded wood shavings? From what I can tell the shavings serve no other function than to act

as filler. Certainly for a cedar scented blend, the shavings are appropriate. What about a Victorian lavender blend or a light spring floral scent? I am reminded of going to a dance in fishing boots when I think of the delicate flowers keeping company with the shavings in the see-through bags.

Potpourri is a plan-ahead project. If you are planning to grow, harvest and dry your own petals and herbs, this is an ongoing project throughout the growing season. You don't have to collect all the ingredients at one time. Dry things as they come into season. Try drying flowers for their beauty as well as for the scent. Although the smaller varieties of zinnia have very little scent, they dry exceptionally well and maintain their color. Give marigolds a try too. Sometimes they fall apart, but that doesn't matter. Potpourri is composed of loose petals as well as entire flower heads. Didn't you have an auntie or granny somewhere along the way who said, "Waste not, want not?" Use it all, busy herb lover.

When I put out the call for reliable blends, the response was overwhelming. The following potpourri blends are collected from and suggested by friends and family. I have listed the "scent families" so that you might know the direction to head scent-wise. Here is a list of leaves, flowers, seeds and spices that are reliable for either outstanding scent or lasting color.

FLOWERS RETAINING COLOR WELL

Lavender	Violets	Chamomile	Pot Marigold
Hollyhock	Roses	Tansy	Strawflowers
Lilac	Yarrow	Statice	Red Clover

DELIGHTFULLY AROMATIC LEAVES

Bay	Lavender	Oregano	Basil
Rosemary	Marjoram	Tarragon	Sweet Woodruff
Lemon Balm	Lemon Thyme	Lemon Verbena	

Geraniums (lemon, spices, rose, mints and others)
Mints (apple, orange, pineapple as well as traditional)
Bergamot (a sweet smelling mint)

SENSATIONAL SPICES

Allspice	Cinnamon sticks	Whole cloves
Vetiver root	Whole nutmeg	Whole ginger

OFTEN OVERLOOKED SEEDS

Star Anise	Coriander

EFFECTIVE ESSENTIAL OILS

Citrus blend	Cinnamon	Lavender	Pine
Lemon	Orange	Patchouli	Sandalwood
Spice Blend	Violet		

Materials:

Large crock or jar with tight fitting lid

Glass or ceramic mixing bowl

Mortar and pestle

Hand grater or hand operated meat grinder for spices

Wooden spoon

Eyedropper

Scoop

Small glass or other attractive see-through containers with lids to use for the aged potpourri.

Preparation:

Gather and dry the necessary ingredients.

Mix herbs, flowers, petals, spices, fixatives in the bowl.

Gently scoop into deep jar or crock.

Add the essential oil.

Stir gently with wooden spoon.

Seal the jar with the cap.

Keep in a cool dark place.

Twice a week gently shake the ingredients by turning the jar or crock upside down then right side up four times.

Do not open the jar for one month.

Scoop into small attractive jars with tops that can be removed to release fragrance into the room and replaced to keep the potpourri fresh until it is needed again.

Reserve a few whole rosebuds or other flower heads to decorate the top of the blend, if you plan to display the potpourri in an attractive open dish.

Hint: When making dry potpourri use only crushed, grated or crumbled spices. If the powdered spices are used, the residue of the powdered spices adheres to the sides of the glass containers leaving a cloudy film, thus spoiling the visual effect.

POTPOURRI BLENDS TO GET YOU STARTED

SPICE SAMPLER
Ingredients:

1 cup rose buds

1 cup mixed flower petals
1/2 cup strawflowers
1/2 cup lemon balm
1/2 cup basil leaves
1/2 cup sage leaves
1/3 cup broken cinnamon sticks
1/4 cup crushed cloves
1/4 cup crushed, dried lemon peel
1 tablespoon lemon oil
1 tablespoon crushed orrisroot

Preparation:
Follow the general directions for making potpourri with dry materials. Store in the recommended manner.

COUNTRY GIRL SPICE
Ingredients:
2 cups rose buds
1 cup rose geranium leaves
1 cup lavender flowers
1 cup strawflowers (assorted colors)
1 whole nutmeg, grated
1/4 cup star anise, crushed
1/4 cup cloves, crushed
1/4 cup broken cinnamon sticks
1 tablespoon orrisroot, crushed
6 drops patchouli oil
4 drops cinnamon oil

Preparation:
Follow the general directions for making potpourri with dried materials. Store as directed.

AUNT EMILY'S VICTORIAN LAVENDER BLEND
Ingredients:
4 cups lavender flowers and spike-like leaves
2 cups thyme
1 cup lemon geranium leaves
1 cup lemon balm
1/4 cup blue statice
4 tablespoons lemon peel, crushed
4 tablespoons whole cloves, crushed
1 tablespoon orrisroot, crushed
4 drops lavender essential oil

Preparation:
Follow the general directions for making potpourri from dry materials. Store in the recommended manner.

SIDNEY'S HINT OF MINT POTPOURRI
Ingredients:
2 cups peppermint leaves
1 cup peppermint geranium leaves
1 cup pennyroyal leaves
1 cup eucalyptus leaves
1 cup bay leaves, crumbled
1/2 cup rosemary
1/2 cup sage leaves
1/4 cup basil
1/3 cup whole cloves, crushed
2 to 4 drops peppermint essential oil

Preparation:
Follow the general directions for making potpourri with dry materials. A note of caution: add peppermint oil one drop at a time. This is a gentle minty mixture. You don't want the house to smell like you are trying to break up chest congestion. Rather than overpower with mint, you can always add more oil later. Store according to directions.

MIDSUMMER MADNESS
Ingredients:
3 cups white and red clover heads
1 cup rosebuds
1 cup chamomile flowers
1 cup blue statice flowers
1/2 cup lavender foliage (spike-like leaves)
1/2 cup wild yarrow flower heads
2 tablespoons whole cloves, crushed
1 tablespoon orrisroot, granulated
2 to 3 drops lavender or other floral essential oil

Preparation:
Follow directions for preparing traditional potpourri from dry ingredients. This is a gentle floral mixture with emphasis on reds/pinks, white, and blue. The clovers and wild yarrow live in fields and by the side of the road and are easily gathered and dried. There is nothing overpowering, and now is your opportunity to experiment with essential oils to develop a personal potpourri fragrance.

ENCHANTED FOREST POTPOURRI
Ingredients:
   3 cups cedar shavings
   3 cups tiny pine cones
   1 cup rosemary
   1 cup bay leaves, crumbled
   1 cup pine needles (balsam tips, hemlock, or pine "tags" from
your yard)
   1 cup white German statice
   1/2 cup whole cloves, crushed
   1 tablespoon orange peel
   1 tablespoon traditional pickling spice
   1 tablespoon orrisroot, crushed
   3 to 4 drops pine essential oil

Preparation:
   Follow the directions for preparing the traditional potpourri from
dry ingredients. You will need to cut or break the pine needles in 1" to
2" lengths. One type of smaller pine cone comes from the white
spruce. If you have access to a hemlock tree, you will have a wealth of
one inch size cones and you should also collect the smaller needles
that inevitably carpet the ground beneath the boughs. If you have no
"yard source," you may also purchase hemlock or white pine cones at
local craft stores or through mail order catalogs.

LAVENDER ROMANCE POTPOURRI
Ingredients:
   2 cups lavender seeds and flowers
   1 cup mixed flower heads and petals
   1/2 cup orange rind
   1/4 cup thyme
   1 tablespoon cloves, crushed
   1 tablespoon star anise, crushed
   1 tablespoon vetiver
   6 drops clove essential oil

Preparation:
   Follow the directions for preparing traditional potpourri from
dried ingredients. Orrisroot may be substituted for vetiver as the fixative.

Simmering Potpourri

In the family of potpourri this variety might be considered the little sister. Not that the development of simmering potpourri is new, but its rise in popularity is fairly recent. The popularity of woodstove inserts in fireplaces has helped promote simmering potpourri. Because the air becomes very dry when an area is heated by a woodstove, water is simmered to keep moisture in the air. Adding peels, rinds, spices, etc. is a pleasant way to aromatically re-hydrate the air.

Setting practicality aside, as the family unit dwindles, the desire for recapturing a nostalgic moment in a less stressful time rises. For whatever reason at some point in every adult life comes a time of reflection and introspection. Is it recovering memories one more time, reaffirming a personal identity? Witness the resurgence in rediscovering, restoring and enlarging old family photographs. People are preserving treasures under glass, putting things in frames like bits of lace, buttons or baby clothing.

Busy herb lover, set aside time to listen to conversations at large flea markets and small garage sales. You will hear, perhaps even say, things like, "We used to have one of these when I was little," or "I remember when my grandmother made such and such with this one summer."

Nostalgia sometimes gets a bad rap as being gooey and overly sentimental. A trip down memory lane triggered by a song or a smell can be a lot of fun and encourage non-threatening, non-judgmental conversation between the generations. One of my brothers smells peanut butter and apple combination and thinks of summer lunches under the shelter in day camp at Wheeling Park. Just as violets take me to the afternoons with my head against my grandmother's ample bosom, listening to her read "The Princess and the Pea," my children to this day say they relate the aroma of bread baking and the smells of sage and cinnamon to coming home from school. I'm happy they've forgotten the gnats flying around the fruit bowl and the moldy cheddar cheese forgotten in the darkest corner of the refrigerator.

Manufacturers must also believe that there is a market for herb and spice scents. The assortment of styles and designs of simmering potpourri "pots" is mind-boggling. There are simple crockery cups warmed by "tea candles." The cost of these ranges from reasonable to expensive. The simmer pot of the nineties also ranges from simple to ornately decorated ceramic, but the warming base is powered by electricity. There are a couple of disadvantages to the electric pot. Always, there is a danger with the electric base of your mixture "simmering dry." If you use the electric pot, you must to be vigilant and add liquid to your preparation occasionally. The other disadvantage is being bound by the electric cord to the location of the outlet.

There is a third option which is usually my option mainly because I am out of time and the occasion is upon me. I mix my ingredients in a sauce pan and simmer on a back burner of my electric range. What to simmer? Open up your spice and herb jars and experiment! You can always open the windows if the scent doesn't please.

SIMMERING POTPOURRI SUGGESTIONS
FESTIVE POTPOURRI
Materials:
Mortar and pestle
Large glass jar with lid
Measuring spoon

Ingredients:
1 tablespoon rosemary
1 tablespoon sage leaves
1 tablespoon thyme
1 tablespoon basil leaves
1 tablespoon orange rind
4 bay leaves

Preparation:
Using the mortar and pestle, crush the herbs
Spoon all the crushed herbs and orange rind into the jar
Tighten the lid and shake to blend.

To Use: Place one tablespoon herb blend for every cup of water into the simmering pot of your choice.

Note: It is possible to use portions of powdered herb, but the results will not be as aromatic. In the crushing of the leaves, oil is released. This oil contributes to the good smell. If you wish, you can add essential oil with the powdered herbs to achieve a good smell.

APPLE SPICE
Materials:
Sharp knife
Cutting board
Mortar and pestle

Ingredients:
1 apple or 1/4 cup dried apple
2 tablespoons whole cloves
2 cinnamon sticks

Preparation:
Remove the skin from the apple and reserve the peel (you may eat the apple flesh).
With the mortar and pestle, crush the cloves
Break the cinnamon sticks into small bits
To Use: Simmer apple, cloves and cinnamon in one cup water. Do not try to use apple or another type of juice. As it evaporates, it leaves a sticky residue. Stay with water as the liquid base.

BEAT THE WINTER BLAHS INSTANT SIMMERING POTPOURRI
Materials:
Measuring cup
1 quart sauce pan
Sharp knife
Cutting board

Ingredients:
1/2 cup assorted dried mint leaves (summer leftovers)
1 orange, lemon or grapefruit (there is usually a piece of fruit which has softened to the point that it is no longer desirable for consumption.)
1 teaspoon powdered cinnamon
1/2 teaspoon powdered cloves
4 cups water

Preparation:
Slice fruit into small wedges.
Combine fruit, herbs and water in the large saucepan.
Bring to a boil, stir then let simmer.

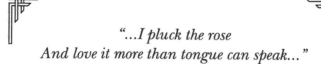

"...I pluck the rose
And love it more than tongue can speak..."

Two in the Campagna
Robert Browning

Sachets

Don't you feel good? You have made your way through the maze of mysterious potpourri terms and assorted preparations! Welcome to the world of sachets, busy herb lover. I look on making sachets as I do Chinese cooking. It is a tastefully delightful way to get rid of leftovers. Did you get a blend that was nice to smell but turned out to be less than "visually delightful?" In other words, you have a mess that smells good, but you don't know what to do with it. Recycle what pleases your nose yet offends your eyes into dainty sachets.

A sachet is nothing more than pot-pourri crumbled to a fine texture then stuffed into a little fabric bag. Not only can you hide your visual mistakes in sachets packets, but also you have the opportunity to use powdered spices. The only limitation you have when making sachets is your imagination.

There is a sachet shape to fit every need. If you wish to have a nice flat packet to slip in among the sheets, towels, or fine linens, create a long flat satin sachet. If you wish something with character for a dresser drawer, make traditional squares adorned with lace. You can create heart shaped sachets from taffeta or animal shapes of calico. You can fashion a little organdy hat or use a traditional drawstring bag.

Sachets are not limited to the dresser drawers and closets. Make a "U" shape to tuck in shoes. How about a decorative sachet to pin to a chair back? Then, there is the ultimate sachet recycling effort. Remember that tooth-fairy pillowcase? The one with the little pocket for the tooth? Freshen a bedroom with a tiny sachet tucked in the tooth pocket.

LOVINGLY LONG PREPARATION METHOD
FOR A SACHET PACKET
Materials:
    Dusty rose colored taffeta
    9 inches of 1/2-inch wide white lace
    Thread to match fabric
    Scissors
    Sheet of polyester filling
    Lavender blend potpourri

Directions:

Cut two 3" x 3" squares of fabric.

Pin gathered edge of ruffle to the edge of one piece of the fabric so that the ruffle lies on the right side of the fabric. Its finished sewing edge must be even with the edge of the fabric.

Pin right sides of the fabric together with the ruffle sandwiched in between.

Sew the sachet evenly on three sides keeping about 1/4 inch margin.

Turn the packet right side out.

Press the square with warm iron. As you press, fold in the raw edge of the fourth side. This will make the final hand closing easier.

Cut 2 small squares of the polyester.

Place the squares of polyester in the bag.

Put 1 tablespoon of finely crushed potpourri in between the layers of polyester. Settle it into the bag so it is not lumpy.

Hand stitch the fourth side to close the opening.

Hint: For a long lasting fragrance carefully place a drop of the essential oil used in the potpourri on the polyester filling as you fill the bag with crushed potpourri.

Variation: Make the sachet packet according to directions. When you prepare to close the fourth side sew a loop of harmonizing ribbon into the seam. This will serve as a loop to hang the sachet on a hook or clothes hanger. If you prefer, crease the ribbon and sew the crease into the seam of the packet. You have two ends to secure the sachet to a location (door knob etc.) and to form a bow.

SACHET FOR SHEETS, TOWELS AND FINE LINENS
Materials:

12 inches of satin-like ribbon or blanket binding at least 4 inches wide

Polyester filler

Rose scented potpourri

Thread to match the fabric

Directions:

Fold ribbon in half so the wrong side is on the outside.

You will have two 6-inch sides.

Stitch the two long sides and leave the narrow end open.

Turn the long rectangle right side out.

Press with a warm iron.

Fold the raw edges in and press for ease in final hand stitching to close the packet.

Slide two strips of polyester fiber into the packet.

Between the layers of polyester place one to two tablespoons of finely crushed potpourri.

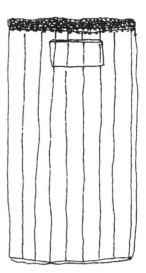

Stitch up the fourth side.

Hint: It is always best when ironing a fabric of unknown composition to try the temperature on a sample before ironing the main item. Handy as they are, steam irons will water stain some fabrics. An iron that is too warm can wrinkle and crinkle a fabric in just one pass over it. Even worse, a hot iron on synthetic fabrics can pick up a gummy residue that will stick on the bottom of the iron and smear over everything before you are even aware it is on the bottom.

BUSY HERB LOVER METHOD
TRUNK OR CHEST SACHET
(USED FOR ITEMS IN LONG TERM STORAGE)
Materials:
　　12" x 18" satin-like fabric
　　13" x 19" lacy fabric
　　Polyester filling
　　Moth repelling potpourri blend
　　Fabric glue

Directions:
　　Spread fabric right side up on a flat surface.

　　Place the lace on top, pin at the four corners.

　　Read the instructions that accompany the glue before you begin the process.

　　Start gluing in the upper left hand corner and continue to spread across the top of the fabric.

　　Smooth the fabric, readjusting the pins if necessary.

　　Glue from the top right corner to the bottom right corner.

　　Glue from the top left corner to the bottom left corner.

　　Continue smoothing as you glue the fourth side.

　　The lace is glued to the fabric so follow the drying instructions.

　　When the fabric and lace are bonded, fold in half to make a 6" x 8" rectangle. The right sides of the lace should be facing each other with the inside of the fabric showing.

Again secure the corners with pins.

Apply the fabric glue to the lace on one 8" side.

Apply the fabric glue to the lace on the other 8" side.

Let the glue dry.

Turn the little pillow right side out.

Saturate the polyester fiber with four drops of pine scented essential oil.

Slide the filler into the pillow.

Place 1/4 cup finely crushed moth repellant potpourri between the layers of polyester filler.

Fold in the rough edges of the opening and glue closed.

MOTH REPELLANT SACHET

Ingredients:

1 cup cedar shavings

1 cup pennyroyal

1/2 cup sweet woodruff

1/2 cup tansy leaves and flower heads

1/2 cup lemon verbena

1/4 cup lemon rind

2 teaspoons ground cloves

3 drops pine essential oil

Preparation:

Follow the directions for making the traditional potpourri from dry ingredients. Remember that this is like all the other potpourris and needs to season for about four weeks before using.

THE BUSY HERB LOVER'S ULTIMATE SACHET

Materials:

Square handkerchief with lace border

1 24-inch length of ribbon (1/2", 1/4" or 1/8" width)

1 to 2 tablespoons of potpourri

Directions:

Carefully press the handkerchief with a warm iron.

Spoon potpourri into the center of the handkerchief.

Draw up the points of the four corners.

Wrap the ribbon two or three times around the fabric above the ball of potpourri.

Tie a bow.

Note: This is a good way to recycle the hand-me-down handkerchiefs of days past. It seems to me as if my assorted great aunties and my grandmother had two types of handkerchiefs, ones they used and ones they perfumed then tucked in the cleavage or tucked near their wrists when wearing long sleeves. My inheritance seems to be a preponderance of "tucking hankies." When in need of an emergency gift or a spontaneous remembrance, I dip into the fathomless supply of lacy handkerchiefs.

Variation: If you have some small plain white or lightly colored handkerchiefs, you could add lace or embroider a simple design, an initial, or perhaps a flower. Use what you have and give it your special touch. If you have nothing on hand, poke around at garage sales, estate sales, and collectable shops for small squares of interesting fabric.

Pomander Balls

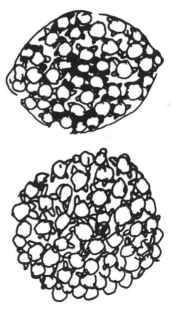

I grew up thinking that pomander balls were designed as traditional holiday work jobs for children while adults were cleaning house, decorating and in general getting ready for the holiday season. Little did I know that throughout history pomander balls were considered a health necessity – although I often claimed to need medical attention as my thumbs grew bruised and tender from pushing cloves into apples.

The original pomanders were designed to ward off plagues, evil spirits and what ever else might be lurking, waiting to attack. An herb preparation was hung about the neck in an ornately designed container. Judges and others working in public places or finding it necessary to venture out in times of pestilence and plague inhaled the aromas from the purifiers.

Today pomanders, although free from the medicinal stigma, are still used as air refreshers. They are hung in closets, displayed in delicate dishes or jars, and often hung on wreaths and adorn trees during the Christmas season. As I mentioned, pomanders are so easy to prepare that even children can make them... without bruising thumbs!

Materials:
   Thin skinned lemon, lime, orange, or apple
   4 ounces of whole cloves
   Pomander rolling mix
   Wooden floral pick or awl
   Thimble
   9" x 13" baking pan

Directions:
   Hint: Work with the pan in your lap. There will be residue from the cloves and sticky juice from the fruit. Consider the fruit as you would our planet earth as you insert the cloves from north pole to south pole.
   To begin, poke one line of holes from top to bottom.
   Insert a whole clove in each hole. (Use a thimble to protect your poking finger.)
   Continue the procedure poking a row at a time spacing the rows close together for an even symmetrical appearance. The fruit that peeks through the clove heads will disappear as the fruit shrinks in the drying process. This method works well not only in spacing the rows but also in cutting down on the excess juice.
   Sprinkle 4 tablespoons pomander preservative mix on ball.
   Rotate the ball as you sprinkle for uniform covering.
   Shake excess into clean pan.
   Repeat process until entire ball has been covered.
   Set aside on a plate to let dry. (about 2 weeks)
   You will know when the fruit is dry because it will shrink, appear nearly weightless, and smell very good.
   Suggestion: To decorate your pomander ball tie it up with ribbon to match your personality or that of the person to whom you wish to give the pomander. You might, as I do when I'm working with pomanders which have been rolled in the preservative mix, place the pomander in the center of a large cotton doily or piece of lacy netting. Draw the material up around the ball and tie with a pretty satin ribbon.

POMANDER ROLLING MIX
Ingredients:
   4 tablespoons powdered cinnamon
   2 tablespoons powdered allspice
   2 tablespoons powdered cloves
   2 tablespoons powdered nutmeg
   1 tablespoon powdered orrisroot

Directions:
   Combine powdered spices in a glass jar.
   Stir until blended.
   Store remaining mix in tightly covered jar.

"From Nature doth emotion come; and moods
of calmness equally are Nature's gift..."

The Prelude
William Wordsworth

"By night we lingered on the lawn,
For underfoot the herb was dry..."

In Memoriam A.H.H.
Alfred, Lord Tennyson

"Open afresh your round of starry folds
Ye ardent marigolds."

I Stood Tiptoe Upon A Little Hill
John Keats

Simple Crafts for All Occasions

Now, herb lover, although you have become acquainted with culinary and aromatic herbs you have yet to embark on the journey into the jungle of crafters. Just as there are authoritative herb gardeners there are hard core crafters who can intimidate you if you let them. The majority of herb and nature craft people are quite friendly and politely competitive. There are those however who guard their secret designs and methods. Early on in my crafting, I did not know about hot glue and glue guns. I naively asked a wreathmaker how she got the sea shells to stick on a grapevine wreath. From her reaction to my question, I thought for certain I had asked her to reveal a secret that would threaten national security. I asked her if she used white glue. Perhaps I had two heads. Was it rubber cement she used? Certainly, I must be speaking the wrong language. This situation passed from interesting to bizarre. Keeping a type of glue a secret!

On another occasion I examined a dried herb and pine cone "flower" wreath at a craft show. Before I learned how to cut pine cones into flowers, before I even knew they could be cut to make flowers, I asked an exhibitor at the craft show if the flowers were wooden. She whooped and then went into something of a high pitched twittering trill, all the while pointing a finger at me and passing knowing looks to those who were attracted by this unaccommodating banshee's howl.

She would not tell me what to use to cut the pine cones, nor would she identify the variety of cone, or even tell if the variety made a difference. When I got nowhere concerning making the flowers, I asked her if she dipped or sprayed the herbs and pine cone flowers to preserve them. The cones had a subtle luster. Perhaps she achieved the shine with hair spray. Her own hair was arranged in a manner that defied gravity.

I have come to find that most hair sprays will work for the moment but do tend to attract moisture especially if you live in a humid climate. I rely on a small amount of clear acrylic spray to preserve and enhance wreaths, baskets and other dried arrangements. I'm sure there is someone out there who has found what he or she believes to be the superior method in doing all things suggested here. What I relay to you, busy herb lover, is what works for me.

All these ideas are meant for you to use as a springboard to your own ideas, designs and creations. How can you begin if you don't know where to begin, what to use, and how to do it at minimal cost for maximum joy? You will see a list of the tools and materials I prefer to use when making the projects in this section. I have included some general information and personal insight into the materials because I am well aware that although the heart is moved by beautiful things, the tool-awareness level does not always match ambitious plans.

Occasionally, you will find a note with a project which requires a specialized tool. If you come across an implement that works better for you, by all means go with it!

Tools, Equipment and Materials

Acrylic Spray (clear): This may be purchased at a craft store. However, the spray paint section of your local discount or hardware store usually has a larger can at a more reasonable price.

Awl: This is a handy tool used for piercing small holes. It is my preference over an ice pick or skewer. I feel less hazardous with the smaller point and sturdy handle. The awl can be found in hardware departments everywhere.

Brush: Small watercolor brushes are handy for a dab of glue in hard to reach places. A brush spreads white glue infinitely better than a toothpick! These little brushes are indispensable for dusting delicate everlastings.

Drop Cloth: Recycle a sheet, shower curtain or plastic tablecloth.

Herbal crafts are messy, and the cleanup is easier when your work surface is covered by a large cloth.

Floral Tape: This tape may be purchased at any craft supply store,
florist or floral supply department of discount stores. It is most commonly found in green although it is available in brown and also in
white. The most common width is 1/2 inch. I have seen it as wide as
two inches. The narrow is good for wrapping wire stems and small styrofoam wreaths.

Gloves: It is your choice when handling pine cones whether you
want to poke your fingers or not. For most projects I do not feel comfortable wearing gloves. Working with pine cones is the big exception.
I prefer the green and gold canvas-like gardening gloves for crafts, for
protection and also flexibility. The lightweight cotton gloves do not
afford much protection.

Glue: There are two traditional glues that work well in crafts when
you don't want to use hot glue. These are white glue and rubber
cement. One advantage of white glue is that many brands are water
soluble and that makes clean up easy. The disadvantage of the water
soluble glue is that if the wreath, basket or other craft is exposed to
much moisture, the glue absorbs moisture and things begin to loosen.
Rubber cement works well and dries fast. A plus for it is that the dry
glue in unwanted areas peels off without leaving a residue or damaging the surface. I use it as an emergency repair glue. It becomes rather
expensive if used in any great quantity. A point to remember is that
the rubber cement will evaporate rapidly if the cap is left off the bottle.

Hot Glue: If you do not have a glue gun, you should invest in one.
There is quite an assortment available. You need to determine what
your needs are and how much money you want to invest. In the case of
purchasing a glue gun the old adage, "you get what you pay for," is
true. The bottom of the line glue gun gives the same results as the
more expensive ones. What is missing is the convenience. Less expensive glue guns require the user to push the glue stick into the barrel
for continuous "feed" to assure a steady flow of glue. The more expensive models have the self-advancing feed. There are cordless glue guns
and those with cords. The choice is yours. There is a petite size that
takes a smaller glue stick, handy for delicate, precise work. I have grad-
uated to a cordless, regular size glue gun and am quite happy. For the
small jobs I use a toothpick, nail or other small pointed item to "dot"
the glue. There is a "cool melt" glue gun available. Its function is
mainly for use with heat sensitive materials such as plastic.

Hot Glue Sticks: Glue sticks are available wherever glue guns are
sold. They are also in home maintenance and repair departments of

many discount stores. A package of 6 or 12 glue sticks looks handy and might do for one project. If you want to do a number of things, you will find it time and money saving to buy in bulk. Craft stores generally sell the big boxes of glue sticks. As a rule, the bulk supply is not on display, so you need to ask for the box. What may seem initially like a big investment will save, over a period of time. Stored properly, glue sticks never go bad. Among the advantages is that hot glue dries quickly and provides a permanent bond. The major disadvantage to hot glue is just that, it is very HOT.

In the beginning as you experiment with hot glue, expect to burn yourself a couple of times. The body of the gun stays reasonably cool, but at the tip where the glue is expelled is intense heat. Because of the heat factor and burn possibility, my advice is to use hot glue with extreme caution and never leave the glue gun with hot glue around small children.

Picks: These are sturdy "over-size" toothpicks pointed on one end. Some picks have wire attached. Typically, the pick color is green. These picks work well when small clusters of herbs or flowers must be securely affixed to a styrofoam or straw wreath base without glue.

Pliers: Long nose pliers are needed for shaping stubborn petals of pine cone flowers. These pliers are also handy for twisting stubborn wire.

Pruning Shears: If you have a pair on hand, fine. If you are going to purchase pruning shears, look carefully because there are several sizes and varieties. Here is where you may want to go for the style and not be concerned with paying a little more. Big doesn't necessarily mean better. Grip the shears in your strong hand. Some shears have something called spring action. Don't be put off by a label that says that the shears are made for women's hands. It seems that leverage is more important than strength with these.

Scissors: Sharp scissors or kitchen shears that are not your sewing scissors. Save your sewing scissors to cut lace and ribbons. These shears are used to cut flower stems and other coarse materials that sometimes dull or pit the blades.

Tweezers: Do not use tweezers that are for personal grooming. Purchase a pair of point end tweezers for the very delicate and intricate placement of items.

U-Pins: These pins look like little croquet wickets. Because of the points on each end, the U-Pin can firmly, securely hold without crushing. They are handy when making fresh herb wreaths using styrofoam or straw base.

Wire: A good supply of assorted wire sizes is a must. The size indicates the flexibility and thickness of the wire. Length has nothing to do with the gage number. The lower the number the thicker, more sturdy it is. In a craft store you will see sizes such as 20, 22, 24 etc. You will also see spools of wire. Keep the low gage sturdy wire for stems and use the flexible green wire for binding "things" to "things."

Wire Cutters: I ruined scissors and pruning shears before I bought wire cutters. It is hard to believe how much damage one little piece of wire can do when it is cut by the wrong tool. Sure, scissors will cut wire, and then they will never cut anything else to your satisfaction. I damaged a perfectly good pair of pruning shears that way. Now they won't cut a vine of any type. What is worse, they resist sharpening.

Wreaths and Wreath Bases

There are several types of wreath bases. They are excelsior, straw, rigid plastic foam, vine and wire. If you think a wreath is a wreath, then think again. Sometimes the base is exactly that, a base. Sometimes the base is an important visual factor in the composition of the wreath. On occasion the base must be a sturdy foundation if the wreath is made from heavy materials. Hopefully, the discussion that follows will help you understand the variety of bases and their assorted uses.

Excelsior: This is a neutral-colored, dainty, almost lacy wreath form. Genuine excelsior is very fine wood shavings. Most excelsior is wrapped around a straw form. Occasionally, you can find a wire-based excelsior wreath. Commercially prepared excelsior wreaths come in assorted sizes. The shapes include heart, oval and round. Excelsior wreaths are available in decorator accent colors. I have made artificial bird nests with excelsior, but I found it was worth my while for larger projects to use "store bought" excelsior wreaths.

Straw: The cost of a straw wreath is minimal so purchasing rather than making is best. The wreath is straw bound to a wire frame with a colorless thread. The popular circle and heart shapes are available in assorted sizes. When selecting a straw wreath, examine it carefully. Each one is different. While the shape may pass inspection, look carefully at the construction. Is it symmetrical? Is it tightly wrapped and firm? Run your hand over the wreath. Is it lumpy and bulging? This may seem like a lot of bother, but it will save you exasperation as you are designing your wreath. Do you wonder if you can remember to examine? It will become automatic, especially if you put out money for a less than satisfactory straw wreath. You may find straw wreaths with plastic coverings. I look on the covering as prepurchase protection and remove it before I decorate the wreath. Usually, I want the straw to be seen as part of the composition. Whether to remove the covering is your decision.

Styrofoam (plastic foam): This is inexpensive and works well for lightweight materials. Plastic foam comes in two colors, white and green. There are hearts, circles, and ovals available in different sizes and widths. Some plastic foam has a rough exterior resembling a rigid sponge. Another variety has a solid smooth appearance. Although it is practical and comes in a variety of sizes and shapes, plastic foam is not visually appealing and works best when wrapped with tape, ribbon or fabric before adorning.

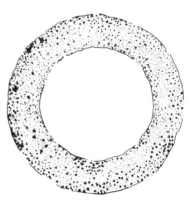

Vine: Many vines are available in the wilds of the backyard. Grapevines are popular and easy to shape. I believe it is healthier for the vine to cut in late fall and winter while the sap is down and no new spring growth has begun. Treat your vine source properly and you will have an abundance of vines for the normal life of the plant. If you hack away at will, eventually you might kill it.

Certainly, do not overlook roadside sources for vines. Honeysuckle grows where nothing else will. I feel no remorse at cutting honeysuckle vines after the sweet blooming in the spring and when it is in its summer foliage. Honeysuckle keeps company on many occasions with poison ivy – NOT a good wreath choice! When in full leaf, both plants are easily identifiable. To the ivy-allergic person, the juice of the poison ivy stem is just as threatening as the leaves.

Honeysuckle is lighter in color than the grapevines. It is more suitable to indoor use as it will mildew when exposed to humidity and the "outdoor elements." Its texture ranges from knobby to smooth. As honeysuckle dries, it sheds a light outer layer revealing a smooth surface beneath. While I believe the shedding adds character to the wreath, others may not.

There is a way to "force-shed" the outer casing of the honeysuckle.

After removing small runners and leaves, coil the honeysuckle as you would rope and simmer on the stove in a large stock pot or roasting pan for approximately two hours. Honeysuckle vine does not have the little curly tendrils of the grapevines, so stripping the outer layer is easy. Take one end of the cooled vine in one hand and pull it through the other hand which is protected by a glove. You may draw the vine through an old towel if you prefer. Anything that a moist honeysuckle vine touches is stained a light brown.

In southeastern Virginia there is an abundance of kudzu vine. I am told it was introduced as a erosion preventive ground cover. In the medians of our highways and interstates the kudzu flourishes undaunted. Along the roadsides it has moved up into the trees. My husband's aunt had kudzu growing on her cliff overlooking the York River. It was planted to prevent the bank from further slipping into the river. She swore, and it was true, the kudzu grew overnight and could creep into the yard without warning. As long as she lived, fighting the kudzu was her ongoing battle. Invariably, an invitation to Sunday dinner also involved a trip over the fence and down the bank to cut back the kudzu.

The redeeming quality of kudzu is that it makes an interesting wreath base. The vine is slender and lends itself to smaller wreaths. It will be a green color as the wreath is shaped. As it dries the bright green fades to a muted tone.

It is fun to design your own vine wreath base, but if you haven't the materials available or are short of time, you can purchase grapevine wreaths in a variety of sizes for a modest price. Sometimes you can find bleached grapevine wreaths. Don't mistake willow for grapevine. The popular willow is somewhat heavier and smoother than grapevine. Quite often the willow wreaths are bleached or painted in trendy decorator colors.

Wire: The assortment of sizes and shapes of wire wreaths is mind-boggling. A single-wire, wire wreath is used when working with Spanish moss, fresh flowers or greens. It is not difficult to shape a circular or heart wreath from a coathanger base. Use a sturdy metal, not plastic coated wire. With the wire cutters, snip off the hook of the hanger. Bend into the desired shape. If all you have available is the plastic coated wire, cut off the hook, cut into the wire to open it into straight lengths. Now twine them together for strength. You must tightly twist the ends together before you work into the desired shape. It is a good idea to cover the wire with floral tape. As you wire things to the base, you will have less aggravation with wire slipping. The uses for the dimensional wire base are limited only by your imagination. It can be filled with moss for a

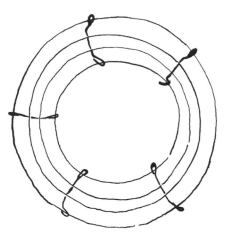

living herb wreath, or adorned with fresh greens for a Christmas decoration. The dimensional wire wreath forms are popular, reasonably priced and available at all craft supply stores.

MAKING A GRAPEVINE OR OTHER VINE WREATH
Materials: (for a 12-inch wreath)

60 feet of grapevine (amount may vary according to vine thickness)

Pruning shears

Gloves (optional)

Instructions:

After you have cut your vines, leave the curly tendrils but nip off any branching off-shoots. You can use the slender extra vine for small wreaths.

Cut the vine into workable lengths. (Eight to ten foot lengths.)

Select the thickest portion of vine for the first loop.

Consider the face of a clock and hold one end of the vine in your left hand at six o'clock.

Bring the vine around clockwise to form a ten inch loop.

Hold the complete loop in your left hand and tuck the beginning end over the newly formed loop to secure the circular shape.

On the second time around, still keeping the idea of the clock, begin an over/under pattern weaving more vine around the first loop.

Begin at the eight o'clock position and weave under the main loop.

Come over the loop at eleven o'clock.

Weave under at one o'clock and so on until you return to six.

The number of over/under motions (usually four to six) depends on the circumference of the wreath.

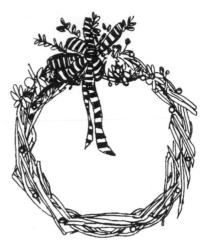

When finishing with one length of vine, tuck and secure the end among the other vine loops.

Continue the weaving beginning "one hour" past your previous starting point.

Work with the vines until the wreath reaches the fullness and width you desire.

Hint 1: Be careful as you weave. It is very easy to whip yourself in the face with the loose ends of the vines.

Hint 2: As you design your wreath, follow the natural movements of the vines. Some vines simply will not be crafted into circular wreaths without soaking and shape forcing on a drying form. I enjoy the personality each batch of vines brings to its shaping. Some of the most attractive wreaths form ovals. Some are almost circular, but one side may not curve as well. When this happens the wreath lends itself to bird nest or other natural arrangement that needs a "shelf" surface.

Note: It saves time and minimizes the transporting hassle if I make the wreath on the spot after I have completed the cutting. There is less likelihood of wasteful overcutting if vines are cut only as needed. Vines are not heavy, but they are an ungainly nuisance to load into a car, getting caught in your hair or snagging a sweater. It is important to form the wreaths from fresh cuttings. Otherwise, the vines become brittle, inflexible and snap – a genuine aggravation. If the vines become too dry, soak them in the bathtub filled with enough warm water to cover them for one to two hours. Some flexibility will return.

MAKING A SPANISH MOSS WREATH BASE
Materials:

Spanish moss (8 ounce package for standard ten to twelve-inch wreath)

Wire base

Drop cloth

Nylon line or monofilament line

Scissors

Note: If you have access to fresh, not packaged, Spanish moss you must "debug" it. Little red bugs and other crawling things maintain secret lives in the moss. Air drying will not do. Fill the bathtub, laundry tub or deep sink with lukewarm water. You will see that the moss comes in strings and strands. Keeping the strands in tact gently dip and "slosh" manageable portions of moss in the water. Hold over the tub and let excess water drip. Spread the moss on newspaper or other absorbent material to drain off any excess water. Arrange thin layers of moss in shallow jelly roll or other wide flat pans. Bake on the warm setting (200 degrees or less) in the oven for about two hours.

Your goal is to rid the moss of bugs without overbaking it. If you do overbake and the moss becomes stiff, there is a chance to revive it by lightly sprinkling or misting with water. As a point of interest, dried Spanish moss strands and stems once were the stuffings of choice for upholstered furniture.

Instructions:

Bend the wire to desired size and shape and twist the ends to secure the form.

Work the moss into several 24 inch lengths.

Firmly but gently wrap the first layer of moss around the form.

Wrap a second thick layer of moss around the form.

With your fingers work the two layers together fluffing and combining them.

Add a third layer of moss if necessary.

When the wreath is the desired size, stabilize it by gently binding the moss with monofilament line.

Variation 1: Wrap a straw wreath base with Spanish moss and secure with the clear monofilament line.

Variation 2: With hot glue bond Spanish moss to the front surface of a vine wreath.

MAKING A SPHAGNUM MOSS WREATH BASE
Materials:

Dimensional wire base
Sphagnum moss
Drop cloth
Monofilament line
Scissors

Note: Sphagnum moss is a form of peat moss. It is the preferred base for a living wreath because the moss will hold moisture and keep your herbs and flowers fresh for a considerable period of time. Sphagnum moss can be purchased from florists and nurseries.

Instructions:

Invert dimensional wire wreath so that the recessed area is up in trough-like position.

Pack generous portions of moist sphagnum moss in the trough.

Work in a clockwise direction until you have filled the trough.

Although the sphagnum moss expands as it is moistened, it may not be packed tightly enough so, as needed, in a clockwise direction fill in sparse spots.

To secure the moss, bind the wreath with monofilament line.

Note: Moisten again if necessary, but do not saturate the moss when you are ready to adorn with herbs and flowers.

MAKING A 14-INCH GERMAN STATICE WREATH BASE

Materials:

Eight-inch single wire wreath base
German statice (four bunches)
Gloves
Floral tape (brown or green)
Floral wire (30 gage)
Drop cloth
Sturdy scissors
Wire cutters

Instructions:

With floral tape, spiral wrap the entire single-wire wreath form, slightly overlapping the tape for a uniform surface.

Spread the drop cloth.

Put on gloves before handling statice. (Tiny stems can splinter and easily penetrate.)

Prepare statice for wiring by cutting flower clusters (approximately three inches in diameter) from the main stem, leaving as much stem on each cluster as possible.

Wrap wire twice around the first cluster.

Keeping the clock face image, with a single wrap around the wreath form, wire the first cluster to the form at 12 o'clock position.

The flowers should point toward 11 o'clock and the stem toward 1 o'clock.

Using continuous wire wrap each cluster once before wiring to the form.

Be careful not to crowd or crush the delicate flowers while fanning the sprigs to the right, the center and the left as they are wired to the base.

The addition of each cluster should hide the stem of the previous cluster as the statice is worked clockwise back to 12 o'clock.

Note: Alone, statice makes a light delicate wreath but is glorious when used as a base to which other flowers or herbs are added. If the plan is to add herbs and flowers, do not be concerned about small gaps in the overall appearance of the wreath. They will be filled!

DECORATING THE UNADORNED WREATH
WITH DRIED HERBS AND FLOWERS

A VINE WREATH FOR THE SPRING SEASON
Materials:
  Oval vine wreath (18 x 14 inch)
  Artemisia
  Spanish moss
  German statice
  Straw flowers in assorted colors
  Tansy buttons
  Yarrow
  Other items with interesting color, texture or shape that you have on hand, such as dried thistles, dusty miller, hydrangea and baby's breath or tiny-headed baby's breath called gypsophilia
  Artificial bird in a pastel color (approximately 4 inches long)
  5 feet of paper twist ribbon (color to correspond with the bird and the available dried items)
  Glue gun
  Hot glue sticks
  Heavy gage floral wire
  Drop cloth

Instructions:
  Arrange a generous amount of Spanish moss on the front and in the bottom arc of the wreath. Only about one quarter of the wreath should be covered.

  Glue the Spanish moss in place by dotting the glue every inch or so on the vine.

  Firmly press the Spanish moss on the glued area, being careful not to push your fingers into the glue.

  Roll an eight inch length of artemisia between the palms of your hands.

  Form the mass into a nest by working it together with your fingers.

  Tuck in some small sprigs of oregano and small curly sage leaves to simulate nesting material in the artemisia.

  Glue the nest in the center of the bottom arc.

Glue the bird into the nest.

Begin with the strawflowers since they are the largest of the flower heads.

Glue one strawflower a thumb width from either side of the nest.

Glue additional strawflowers spaced in the moss.

Glue clusters of statice between and around the strawflowers.

Periodically as you work, stand back and check the overall appearance of the wreath.

Fill in spaces with tansy buttons and yarrow.

Glue the bow to the top arc of the wreath.

Position the bow's streamers, gracefully draping them along the sides of the wreath.

Secure the streamers with dots of glue.

Sparingly apply acrylic spray.

Hint 1: Three very short bursts of spray will usually do it. This is applied as a fixative and not meant to create a heavily lacquered look.

Hint 2: Forget the idea on this wreath that more is better. Crowding the delicate herbs and flowers diminishes the individual charms.

MAKING A DOUBLE LOOP TWIST
PAPER BOW FOR THE SPRING WREATH
Instructions:

Cut a 32-inch length of paper twist ribbon which is in the original twist.

Unroll and smooth the twist paper ribbon.

Without cutting, measure 16 inches.

Glue the free end to the 16 inch mark in order to create and secure the loop which will be eight inches in diameter.

Make a second loop.

Glue the final free end to the loop.

Unroll the remaining 28 inches of ribbon.

At the halfway mark fold both side edges of ribbon to the center creating a one inch strip.

Pinch the bow loops in the center and to secure the loops, bind with a small length of 30 gage wire.

To secure the bow, tie the long length of ribbon around the middle of the loops over the wire but working the wire ends free to attach to the wreath.

Spread the bow loops to give a butterfly wing illusion.

Attach to the wreath as directed.

Hint: To prepare for work with the paper twist ribbon, rub lotion or petroleum jelly into your fingertips. The ribbon dries the fingers so quickly. After working with the ribbon, wash your hands and apply more skin lotion.

Variation: Recycle! Look around at the treasures of your home. You may have wooden eggs, miniature wire garden furniture, an artificial bunny to peek through the flowers, or other "spring" items that you could nestle in the arc of the wreath in place of the bird. Adjust the color of the paper twist ribbon and the arrangement of herbs and flowers to suit your design.

A VICTORIAN THEME FOR SPANISH MOSS WREATH
LOVINGLY LONG METHOD
Materials:

Spanish moss wreath base (12-inch diameter)
Dried pink and deep red rosebuds
Heather
Sage sprigs
Lavender sprigs
Rosemary sprigs
Eucalyptus
Bleached baby's breath (this is a creamy white as opposed to the natural beige color)
German statice
3 yards satin finish antique rose colored ribbon (2 inch wide)
1 yard off-white lace ribbon (2 inch wide)
Drop cloth
Floral tape (white)
Floral wire (30 gage)
Floral picks
Scissors
Wire Cutter
Glue gun and hot glue sticks

Instructions:

Spread the drop cloth.
Spread out dried materials in small bunches across the drop cloth.

Draping the ribbon:

Consider the shape of the Spanish moss wreath because a less opulent area is the ideal spot for the six inch diameter bow.

Cut two yards of the satin finish ribbon. (Reserve one yard for the bow, and use two yards for draping the wreath.)

Apply glue to the end of the ribbon.

Press ribbon end gently into the area of the moss selected for the bow.

This is not a binding of the wreath, rather it is a gentle looping to adorn the front surface.

In six inch sections dot the ribbon with glue beginning on the underside then applying the dot of glue on the top side of the ribbon at the next six inch interval. This gives a gentle looping twist to the ribbon.

After the draping is completed, check the overall effect. You may wish to go around the wreath again, pressing the ribbon into the moss at approximately three inch intervals, working back to the starting point. This will give a closer drape, a more compact look. Never glue the ribbon until you are completely happy with the drape.

Adorning the wreath:

After you have sorted and selected the herbs and rosebuds, bind with the wire small clusters of the herbs to the picks.

By spiral wrapping, cover the wire, stems and picks with white floral tape.

Consider the clock image in adorning.

The bow will be positioned at six o'clock.

Insert a grouping of three rosebuds at twelve o'clock.

Arrange and insert similar clusters at nine and three o'clock.

Work your arranging from the focal point at twelve down to nine and three.

Begin by removing large eucalyptus leaves from the stems, then carefully glue in around the rosebuds to simulate leaves.

Working with one herb at a time, position around the ribbon and in the open areas. At this point extend the dried materials to the eight and four o'clock positions. You may arrange around the draped ribbon. At the points where the ribbon is glued to the moss, you may wish to arrange the dried material to cover the glued spot.

Insert the picks with the dried herbs bound to them into position.

Add German statice and baby's breath where needed. (Here is the opportunity to put your creative eye to use. A delicate, romantic look for this particular wreath cannot be achieved if the moss is completely covered and the dried herbs and flowers are packed tightly together.)

Insert the pick holding the bow at the six o'clock position.

At the center of the bow fan out in a circle small clusters of baby's breath to make a nest for a large rosebud.

Glue rosebud into the center of a halo of baby's breath.

Hint 1: By gently removing your dried herbs and flowers from the storage containers you can see sizes and shapes without damaging the material.

Hint 2: The top of this wreath is the focal point. Use larger, more colorful materials at the top gradually tapering quantity and quality as you move down the sides. All dried things are not perfect but can be used successfully when strategically placed. Don't waste anything. If damage does occur rendering some of your dried things useless for arrangements, simply add the discards to your potpourri blends.

Variation: Omit the lace and use a deep wine, almost garnet color, and choose rosebuds of a deep, purpley red.

MAKING THE TRADITIONAL TWO-LOOP BOW

You may choose to glue the lace to the satin ribbon to give the illusion of all one ribbon. I prefer to have the lace and satin loops independent of each other so the directions that follow will produce the effect of two satin and two lace loops with streamers.

Instructions:

Holding the lace on top of the satin finish ribbon, tie a loose knot at the 18 inch mark.

Using the traditional "tying your shoe lace" method, tie a bow.

Work the loops until they are the desired size.

Insert a wire through the knot behind the loops.

Twist both ends of the wire around a floral pick.

Insert the pick in the desired location.

If you wish shorter streamers from the bow, cut them.

Lightly apply acrylic spray to the entire wreath.

Hint 1: Stuff the loops of the bow with tissue paper before spraying. The acrylic spray will give body to the bow. Leave the tissue in the loops until the spray has dried.

Hint 2: Taffeta-look ribbon with wired edges is available if you prefer a bow that you can bend into position.

THE BUSY HERB LOVER METHOD
FOR ADORNING A SPANISH MOSS WREATH

Instructions:

Select the herbs, flowers, and ribbon as suggested in the "Lovingly Long Method." Instead of affixing the dried materials to picks and taping the picks, use hot glue to bond the materials directly into the moss.

Make the bow the same way but glue it into the moss.

Note: Using the hot glue method, you can assemble this wreath in very short time. The major drawback is that you won't be able to take the wreath apart and rework it for another season or event. If you are putting together a lovely gift and the deadline is looming, hot glue is the answer.

CREATING AN HEIRLOOM STYLE STATICE-BASE WREATH
Materials:

The following dried flowers and herbs: Zinnias (pink and purple), lavender head blossoms, statice (purple or blue), sage, oregano, rosemary, tansy buttons, yarrow

Statice wreath
Drop cloth
Hot glue gun and glue sticks
Scissors
Medium gage wire for hanger
Wire cutter

Instructions:

Using the clock face illusion, place selected zinnias at twelve, three, six and nine o'clock.

Consider the base points and in zig-zag fashion arrange more zinnias around the face of the clock/wreath.

Glue the lavender blossom heads on each side of the zinnias.

Separate sage leaves, touch the stem end with a dot of glue and nestle among the statice clusters, adding sage all around the face of the wreath in a random pattern.

Glue tansy buttons among the statice clusters.

The yarrow is larger than the tansy and other herbs, so add as needed for balance and eye appeal.

Add the remaining herb sprigs, one variety at a time until you are satisfied with the wreath.

Do not use a bow on this natural wreath!

Note: Statice is the base of the wreath, so you need not be concerned about covering it. Rather look on it as a medium to showcase your dried herbs and flowers.

Variation: If you make this statice wreath during the summer months, you have the option of fresh herbs and flowers. Don't dry or glue them. Gently tuck them in among the statice clusters and let them air dry as you enjoy your wreath.

ADORNING WREATHS USING FRESH HERBS

DESIGNING A SPHAGNUM MOSS WREATH
WITH LIVING HERBS
Materials:
Drop cloth
Sharp knife
Medium gage floral wire for wreath hanger
Wire cutters
Sphagnum moss wreath (packed, moistened, prepared for planting)
Two plants each of the following variety of culinary herbs:
Lemon thyme, creeping winter savory, rosemary, marjoram
OR
Rosemary, creeping basil, parsley, oregano
OR
Assorted mints including apple, orange, pineapple and lemon balm
OR
Assorted varieties of thyme

Instructions:
If you wish this to be a hanging wreath instead of a centerpiece, cut a ten inch length of wire for the hanger.

Firmly bend the wire in half.

Using the pliers, grip the two ends of the wire.

Take the loop in your other hand and in three complete twists turn the wire into a two inch loop leaving two inch ends.

With pliers twist the loose ends of the loop around the raised center support wire on the back of the wreath.

Remove enough moss, using the knife if necessary to cut through moss thickness, to provide space to plant herb roots and some of the original potting material. Set the excess moss aside. Remove only one plant at a time from its pot. It is not good to have the roots exposed.

Tap container to free the herb. Be prepared, moving the plant sometimes traumatizes it. Occasionally a plant gets severe droop after replanting. It should spring back in 24 to 48 hours. If you pull the plant out of the pot by the stem, you might bruise it. After the holes are prepared, insert each plant into the moss at intervals.

Break up excess moss and gently repack around the plant as needed.

Add water as needed to keep the moss moist. The moss holds moisture for long periods of time so there is no need to keep it so saturated with water that it is dripping.

Hint 1: Use the fresh herbs on the living wreath for culinary needs. It is an interesting conversational attraction for dinner guests to snip fresh herbs to garnish their salads.

Hint 2: If you prepare this wreath for gift giving, attach small scissors on a colorful ribbon and a note encouraging use and care of the living gift.

Variation: Prepare the living wreath using mints, scented geraniums and other tea herbs. You can snip fresh herbs for hot or iced tea. Encourage guests to prepare individual blends on the spot.

THE BUSY HERB LOVER'S METHOD OF PREPARING A SPHAGNUM MOSS WREATH WITH FRESH HERBS

Materials:
Drop cloth
Small sphagnum moss wreath
Fresh herb cuttings
Boxwood or other greenery
Medium gage florist wire
Wire cutters
Pliers

Instructions:
Work on the drop cloth.
Prepare a hanging loop from the florist wire.
Position the hanger and twist into place on the back of the wreath.
In the moist moss, poke your finger to make a small hole.
In each hole insert sprigs of fresh herbs, boxwood and what other cuttings you might have.

Note: This is not a living, growing wreath. To prolong the beauty of the wreath, mist the foliage with water every day as well as keeping the moss moist. The herbs will not miraculously grow roots; after three to four weeks they will need replenishing with fresh ones if you want to continue to have a fresh wreath.

PREPARING A FRESH HERB CULINARY WREATH USING A WIRE BASE

Materials:
Drop cloth
Lightweight florist wire
Wire cutters
Six inch triple wire wreath form
Assorted fresh culinary herbs

Instructions:

Spread the drop cloth.

Prepare bundles of fresh herbs (mixed together or bundled according to variety).

Wrap each bundle three times with the wire.

Using the florist wire bind the bundles to the center support of wire frame.

Continue layering the herb bundles around the wreath in clockwise direction until the wreath is full and appealing to the eye.

You may suspend this wreath by a ribbon from its hanging loop, but do not use a bow on this wreath.

Hint 1: Herbs range in color from dark green to gray. There are also herbs with variegated foliage. Look at the variety of thymes, sages, and basils for bright spots of color.

Hint 2: Why not spice up your herb wreath by wiring stick cinnamon and individual nutmegs among the bundles? If your wreath is sizeable, do not overlook the use of small whole garlic or individual garlic cloves to add variety.

Note: In giving any culinary wreath, include recipes or a little folklore concerning the contents of the wreath.

NON-EDIBLE SPICE WREATHS MADE ON PLASTIC FOAM BASES

LAUREL WREATH
(A GIFT TO COMMEMORATE ACCOMPLISHMENT)

Materials:

    12-inch foam wreath

    Floral tape (green or brown)

    1 ounce bay leaves (leaf size varies)

    White glue

    Straight pins

    6 feet of plaid or print ribbon (muted, earthy tone colors work well)

    Medium gage floral wire

    Glue gun and hot glue

    Wire cutters

Instructions:

Using the overlap wrap method cover the wreath base with floral tape.

From the wire, form a hanging loop.

Position the loop on the back of the wreath at 12 o'clock.

Bond with a generous amount of hot glue.

After the glue dries turn the wreath base over.

Again considering the clock face, begin at 12 o'clock.

Spread white glue from 12 to 2 as the clock face goes.

Select three bay leaves of uniform size.

Stack the leaves one on top of the other.

Carefully insert a straight pin through the first stack of leaves one quarter of the way down the leaves from the stem end.

Pin the bay leaf stack into the foam base on the glue at the 12 o'clock mark.

Carefully fan the three leaves.

This will give a pattern to follow when gluing the remainder of the leaves, until coming full circle back to the 12 o'clock starting point.

There is no need to pin any other leaves unless for some reason they are not staying in position as they dry.

Cover wreath with a layer of waxed paper and use a book or other heavy object to press the leaves until the glue dries.

The drying process, depending on the amount of humidity in the air, takes about 12 hours.

Add a multi-loop bow at the 12 o'clock position (instructions for making this bow are found with "A Swag From Herbs").

Hint: Positioning and gluing three leaves at a time allows for adjustment if you look back over the leaves and need to reposition. You will sense a rhythm developing if you keep in mind as you position the leaves; side, side, center, side, side, center.

Variation 1: Adorn the bay leaves with one or more of the following: bits of broken cinnamon sticks and whole cloves, whole allspice, coriander seeds, dried rose hips or dried cranberries.

Variation 2: Use the bay leaf base and adorn with dried apple wedges or rings, two-inch cinnamon sticks, cloves and whole nutmegs.

COUNTRY COUSIN SPICY BEAN WREATH
Materials:

Drop cloth
6 inch foam wreath
Brown floral tape
White glue
Glue gun and hot glue
Medium gauge floral wire for wreath hanger

Small jars to hold extra beans
Awl
Cloves
Bay leaves
A variety of dried beans: navy, red, pinto etc.
Split peas (yellow and green)
Crushed red pepper
Chopped chives
Dill seed

Instructions:

Wrap foam wreath in overlap method with floral tape so that no color shows through the tape.

You will be "planting" two rows of cloves around the edge of the wreath. To accomplish this, begin with three holes side by side along the bottom edge on one side of the wreath. Insert one clove in each hole. Note the fit. Are they close enough together to make an even line? Are they too close? Experiment with spacing and filling before poking holes all the way around the wreath edges. The object is to stud with double rows of cloves the interior and exterior sides of the wreath.

After the clove studding is completed, select the bay leaves you will use for the base layer of the wreath.

Plan to arrange and glue one quarter of the wreath at a time.

Arrange the bay leaves so they lay end to end, overlap and extend beyond the edge of the wreath.

Place waxed paper on the leaves, weight with a book while the glue dries.

Carefully spread white glue over the bay leaves and arrange red beans around the wreath in a solid layer.

Press with the palm of your hand to keep an even surface.

Without waiting for the glue to dry, add a layer of navy beans over the red beans.

Gently press this layer to shape a flat surface.

Let the glue dry for about an hour.

Spread glue over the navy beans and add a layer of pinto beans.

The beans will be mounding by this time so again, still preserving the mound, gently press to give a uniform surface.

Spread glue across the top of the mound and sprinkle a layer with a mixture of dried peas.

The excess that falls off can be "resprinkled."

Place waxed paper on top of the bean wreath and weight it down again.

Let dry overnight.

Spread a generous layer of white glue across the top of the beans.

For the final layers add first the chives, then red pepper and finally dill seed.

With glue gun and hot glue bond a wire loop to the back of the wreath for the hanger.

Note: While this would appear to be a messy, time consuming project, it is fun. Be creative in the use of assorted beans, the results are different every time. This project is well suited to the busy herb lover because it can be done in stages. I keep everything together on a large serving tray that can be put out of sight and brought back out in a moment's notice. I can also do two or three at a time because of the various stages.

THE BUSY HERB LOVER METHOD FOR A MINI SPICE WREATH

Materials:

9" x 13" x 2" baking pan

3-inch firm plastic foam ring

White glue

Small watercolor paint brush or wooden match stick for spreading glue

Dill seed, mustard seed, whole allspice, a mixture of powdered spices or a blend of crushed dry herbs (parsley, oregano, rosemary, basil, thyme etc)

1/4-inch ribbon (12 inches long)

Instructions:

Spread glue on interior surface of the ring.

Sprinkle selected spice or herbs on interior surface in quantity to coat the area.

Spread a layer of glue on one side of the wreath.

Pour on the herbs and pat them into the glue.

Set aside to dry for 15 minutes.

Gently shake off any loose seeds or herbs and turn over the wreath.

Spread a layer of glue on the other side.

Repeat the patting procedure.

Let dry for 15 minutes.

Finally, coat the outer rim of the little form with glue.

Roll the little form through the seeds or herbs in the pan until the outer edge is well coated.

Let this dry for 2 hours.

At the end of the drying period, check for bare spots.

Dot the bare spots with glue and pat on more seeds or herbs.

Tie a loop of narrow ribbon around the little wreath to serve as a hanger.

Hint: Make a little shoelace two-loop bow and with a straight pin, affix it to the top of the outer edge. Try pinning the hanging loop instead of tying it around the wreath.

Decorating with Fresh Herbs and Flowers

A SWAG FROM HERBS

A swag is a rope decorated with flowers. Swags fall from decorating grace and then they are rediscovered. They are popular at holiday time but can cater to any season or event by composition. Swags can adorn mantels, lounge above doorways and over windows. They may be made from fresh or dried materials. Since there is no way to keep the herbs and flowers moist, the life of a fresh swag with the exception of a pine-bough based swag is limited. The ones composed of dried flowers can last for years if cared for and stored properly.

Materials:

Drop cloth

Medium weight floral wire

Wire cutters

Gloves

Rope

Assorted dried herbs and flowers (German statice, blue statice, dusty miller, silver king artemisia, lambs ear, strawflowers, clover, daisies, tansy buttons, yarrow, baby's breath, sage, oregano, rosemary etc.)

2 yards of ribbon

Scissors

Instructions:

Identify the size space where you will use/hang the swag.

If it is a three foot space, cut six feet of rope.

With floral wire bind each end of the rope to form a loop about the size of a woman's fist. Use these loops to hang the swag or simply as ornamental and attach the bows to them.

Decide if you want a regular repeating pattern with each bundle prepared in identical fashion, or you would like free form with the "natural" look.

Select the materials for three bundles. Trim the excess stems if needed. The length of the bundle, counting the stems, should not exceed six inches.

Prepare one bundle and wrap the stems three times with wire.

Prepare two additional bundles.

Working from left to right, beginning just past the end loop position the bundle so the stems point towards the center, then wire the bundle.

Overlap as you would on the wire wreath and bind the stems of the next bundle to the rope with two wraps of the wire.

Repeat the wiring process with the third bundle.

Now, look at the design that is forming. It is not yet the point of no return – you can still change the arrangement.

Proceed with making three more bundles of dry materials; three at a time is suggested so you can see your progress and assess your needs at short intervals.

Continue with this procedure until the rope is covered from knot to knot. Triple wrap the final cluster. The stems can be trimmed then covered with the bow.

Prepare two multi-loop bows.

Attach one bow to each end of the swag at the knots.

Variation 1: If this is a small delicate swag to adorn a bride's chair, a birthday "throne" or an infant's cradle, consider dusty miller, roses on stabilized wire stems, baby's breath, and rosemary as the basic components of each bundle. Add to this as the occasion warrants. Plan to use ribbon the width of one-eighth inch in two or three colors. Work the narrow ribbons among the bundles as well as affixing the tri-color, multi-loop bows at each end.

Variation 2: Prepare a small herb swag to adorn a kitchen window or door frame.

Christmas Variation 1: It is cost efficient and quick to make this swag when fresh pine, holly sprigs, boxwood and other greenery is added. Although this swag can be designed for larger spaces, know that it will need several support hooks or nails to drape because of the increased weight. It is easier to complete the Christmas swag in two steps. First, wire bunches of greenery. Small pine cones are optional. Second, add the dried herbs and flowers. Sage and rosemary give off a pleasingly fresh aroma. Statice, strawflowers and baby's breath work well as colorful fillers. Add a multi-loop bow of red velvet on either end of the Christmas swag.

Christmas Variation 2: Begin with the greenery suggested in Christmas Variation 1. Add clusters of dried apple wedges, cinnamon sticks, whole nutmegs, white statice and baby's breath. Use red plaid ribbon for the multi-loop bows with long streamers. In addition to placing bows on either end of the swag, also place bows at the draping points. The cinnamon and nutmeg will "spice up" the air.

MAKING A MULTI-LOOP BOW
Materials:
Ribbon (You will need approximately four yards – or more, if you wish to twine extra through the swag)
Scissors
Lightweight floral wire
Wire cutters

Instructions:
Make a 10-inch circle of ribbon. Hold the first loop between your thumb and forefinger.

Continue looping the ribbon until you have eight or ten loops.

Wrap the floral wire twice around the center of the ribbon.

Twist it tight and cut, leaving five inches of free wire to bind the ribbon to the rope.

Cut four 18-inch lengths of ribbon.

Gather the four lengths, one on top of the other, and tie them around the center of the loops, covering the wire but freeing the end of wire designated for use to bind the bow to the rope.

With your finger, loosen the loops by gently moving one loop forward, the next one back and so on until all the loops are free.

TITANIA'S MIDSUMMER'S NIGHT KISSING BALL
Materials:
Drop cloth
18-inch length of heavy gage wire
Wire cutters
Pliers
Scissors
Awl
Foam ball (12 inch circumference)
White glue
Wooden matchstick or toothpick
Glue gun and hot glue

Ribbon to accent the flowers (1/2" or 3/4" width works well)
German statice (dried)
Blue annual statice (dried)
Dark red rosebuds (dried)
Tiny-headed baby's breath (gypsophilia, dried)
Fresh herbs: lavender, thyme, sage, rosemary, oregano (each herb
cutting should be about 6 inches long)

Instructions for preparing the form:
Bend the wire in half forming a "U."
Push the ends of the wire into the top of the ball and through the
ball so they come out the under side.
Twist the exposed ends to form a loop on the underside (one loop
serves to secure the bow while the other loop will be used to hold the
hanging ribbon.)

Instructions for adorning the ball:
Cut tiny sprays consisting of three or four branches of German statice from the main bunch – later you will use individual branches of
the tiny flowers as more filler for bare spots.
Consider the ball as a globe with the imaginary equator line passing around the middle as you use the awl to poke small holes for the
tiny sprays of statice.
With a gentle touch so you won't dent the plastic foam ball, poke
three holes on the imaginary equator at approximately one half inch
intervals. (This will give you the opportunity to figure the spacing that
best fits your materials. The first couple of holes and "plantings" are
experimental to see how much of the sturdy stem needs to be cut off
so the statice will be nearly flush with the surface of the ball.)
After a trial fitting and trimming, the statice is ready to "plant."
With a matchstick or other small pointed object insert a dot of
glue into the hole.
Insert the stem-trimmed branch of statice.
Continue this procedure around the circumference of the ball.
Using the original row as a guide, prepare rows on either side,
gradually working in smaller circles until finally reaching the support
wires.
Let glue dry and allow the arrangement to set up for about four
hours.
Fill in any obvious bare spots at this time by gluing and inserting
single branches in the empty spaces. (If you try to do this before original arrangement dries, you will have a mess, branches will drop out,
glue will ooze onto the statice.)

Scatter the blue statice around the ball. It has strong stems and should be glued and inserted in the same way as the German statice.

Prepare seven generous clusters of oregano and thyme by gathering them in your hand, binding the stems with floral tape, trimming long uneven stems. You do not need to use wire to stabilize these small bundles.

As directed with the statice, using the awl, poke holes in the ball, glue and insert the clusters of fresh herbs.

Work the long sprigs of oregano and thyme through the statice to create a twining effect.

Insert sprigs of lavender and rosemary in glue-filled prepared holes wherever they seem to fit.

The hot glue will be used for the rosebuds and tiny head baby's breath.

Working with one side of the ball, position the rosebuds (perhaps in a zig-zag fashion around the imaginary equator).

Circle the base of a rosebud nestled with two small sprigs of tiny head baby's breath with hot glue and insert in the preplanned position among the herbs and statice.

Continue this way until all the rosebuds are bonded to the material that surrounds them.

Let the entire ball dry overnight.

Repair, fill in, adjust anything that needs it.

Make a four loop bow with long streamers.

Tie this bow to the bottom wire.

Run a length of ribbon (determined by you according to the use) through the top loop of the ball for suspending it from an overhead hook or chandelier.

Note: Do not use hot glue directly on the foam base. The hot glue will melt the foam. White glue is too heavy and slow drying to be used to hold rosebuds and baby's breath in place.

Hint: As the herbs dry, they will shrink. To refresh your ball simply weave more fresh herb through the statice or try making small ribbon bows, affixing them with hot glue in places that need "perking up."

Christmas Variation: It is simple to convert the summer decoration to a Christmas theme. Insert boxwood and statice into the ball according to the directions. Use mistletoe, baby's breath, red and white straw flowers, miniature pine cones and Christmas print, plaid or red velvet ribbon.

"HATS OFF TO SPRING" WALL OR DOOR DECORATION
Materials:

Drop cloth
Medium gage floral wire
Glue gun and hot glue
Wire cutters
Scissors
Wide brim hat
2 yards pastel ribbon (2 inches wide)
Beige lace (2 1/2 inches wide flat lace not gathered)
Spanish moss
Strawflowers
White statice
Purple statice
Baby's breath
Lavender (dried sprigs and flowers)

Instructions:

Measure the distance around the exterior of the hat where the crown meets the brim.

Cut a length of pastel ribbon to circle the crown.

With hot glue, glue the ribbon around the crown of the hat overlapping about one half inch. You will be working from the edge of the brim in towards the crown as you add the lace. Measure a width of the lace in from the edge. If you are using two inch lace, two inches in from the brim is the starting place for making the first layer of the two-layer lace trim on the brim of the hat. It is best not to cut the flat lace, until you see how deep you want the gathers, and the way the lace lends itself to the process. The object is to make gentle folds in the lace, not gather it as you would a ruffle.

For consistency the starting and finishing spot should correspond with the overlap of the crown ribbon. Spread a six-inch line of glue

(work in small sections so you can
get the effect you want before the
glue dries).

Carefully place two inches of
the lace edge in the glue.

At the two-inch mark, overlap
the lace border (this will resemble
a fold) in a one-half inch overlap
and press into the glue. Continue
the spread "two inch, fold overlap
one-half an inch and glue" procedure around the hat.

Cut the lace to overlap about
one-half inch.

Following the directions for
the first layer, glue a second layer
of lace. Keep in mind as you add
the second layer of lace that the
edge of the second layer must
cover the glued edge of the first
layer.

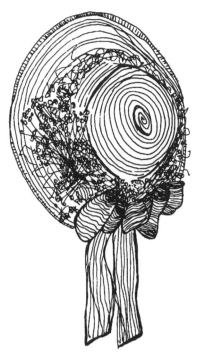

Arrange and glue Spanish
moss around the crown, spreading
it to cover the glued edge of the second layer of lace.

Arrange the strawflowers around three-fourths of the brim.

The ribbon will be positioned in the moss-covered, unadorned
area.

Arrange groups of three strawflowers at twelve o'clock, three
o'clock and nine o'clock.

Work in clusters of statice and baby's breath in the spaces between
the strawflowers.

Add lavender flowers where subtle color is needed.

Make a double loop lace and ribbon bow.

Glue the bow into position.

Make a wire hanger loop and glue it on the underside of the brim
about half way between the edge of the brim and the crown.

Directions for making the traditional double loop bow can be
found with the Victorian theme moss wreath.

Variation 1: Instead of putting lace on top of the brim, using hot
glue, glue a single layer of one inch wide ruffled eyelet lace on the
underside of the brim so it peeks out. Adorn the top with the dried
materials.

Variation 2: For the special luncheon or dinner, adorn miniature straw hats with ribbons and bows. Make tiny net bags filled with pot-pourri and glue them inside the crown of the hat. Add a strip of magnetic tape and turn the party favor into a refrigerator magnet.

BUSY HERB LOVER METHOD
FOR SUMMER HAT CENTERPIECE
Materials:
   Broad brim summer hat
   Daisies
   Fresh thyme

Instructions:
   Wash the thyme cuttings and set aside until dry.
   Arrange a thick layer of fresh thyme around the brim of the hat.
   Tuck daisies into the thyme.
   Note: There is no glue involved which means the hat must lie flat otherwise the decorations will fall off. After the party, recycle the thyme by rewashing it if necessary and hanging it to dry for other uses.

SEASON OF MELLOW FRUITFULNESS DECORATED BASKET
Materials:
   Drop cloth
   Work gloves
   Glue gun and hot glue sticks
   Pruning shears
   Needle nose pliers
   Scissors
   Spanish moss or silver artemisia
   Baby's breath
   Small pine cones
   Medium pine cones cut into 8 flowers
   Assorted nuts -acorn, hazelnut, pecan (in the shell)
   Cinnamon sticks
   Whole cloves
   Apple slices (dried)
   Tansy buttons (dark gold to brown tones)
   Sage sprigs (dried)
   Woven basket of grapevine or twig (about 10 inches in diameter)

Making pine cone flowers:
   Because cutting the pine cones is a messy job, outside is the place to work. The size of the pine cone determines the number of flowers cut from it. Do not forget to put on gloves for handling the pine

cones! You might get thorny-type splinters in your fingers or pine tar on your hands.

Starting with the small end, cut off the top one fourth of the way down the cone. What emerges looks like an opening flower. To prepare the pine cone flowers for arrangements in baskets or other containers instead of basket borders, wire them, creating stems that can be covered with floral tape.

Cut the remainder of the pine cone in half by working the shears in between layers towards the center core. This takes some muscle. The first few cutting times can be frustrating. Stick with it, you will be pleased with the results. If you are lucky, the bottom half will not split, and you will have two rough, unfinished "flowers."

To finish the flowers use the needle nose pliers to pick away broken pine cone "petals."

The flower will resemble a zinnia.

The third section of the pine cone flower will be the largest. Work on it just as you did the other, picking away the broken "petals." A tufty center will emerge. Pick at it to the point that it looks like it has porous texture.

Decorating the basket:

Separate your materials into piles on the drop cloth.

With hot glue, replace any acorn "caps" that are loose.

Spread out the Spanish moss or artemisia into strips.

Dot hot glue over one quarter of the basket edge.

Arrange the Spanish moss or artemisia over the glued area, pressing gently while arranging.

Continue this procedure until the entire basket rim is covered.

Place two sets of three pine cone flowers (large in the center flanked by two smaller flowers) on opposite edges of the basket (12 o'clock and 6 o'clock on the face of a clock).

At 2 and 4, 8 and 10 o'clock marks space a small flower or the first cut which resembles the opening flower.

At this point evaluate the decorations to decide if the basket should be completely decorated around the rim with pine cones, nuts. etc. For a lighter touch use more baby's breath as filler and less nuts, This seasonal basket is appropriate from early fall through the winter holidays.

After the evaluation, proceed with decorating.

Glue into place the pine cone flowers.

Make clusters of two or three acorns or other nuts and glue into desired position.

Glue sprigs of baby's breath in bare spots.

Some sample
baskets for
gift giving...

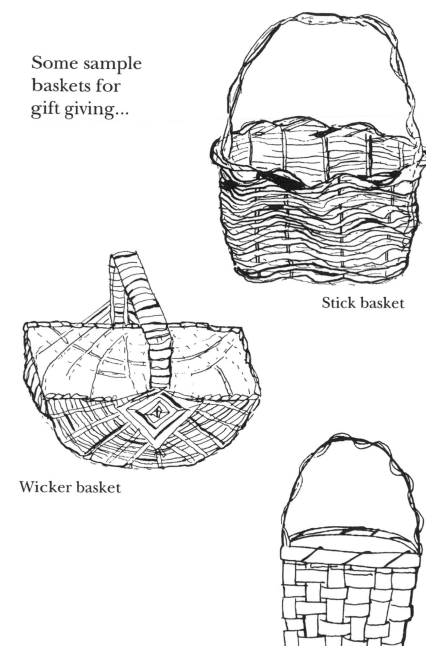

Stick basket

Wicker basket

Reed basket

Trim herb stems.
Accent the basic decoration with dried herbs.
Glue on dried apples.
Tuck three or four whole cloves around the nuts.
Crunch a cinnamon stick with the bottom of a glass.
Glue the slivers of cinnamon stick at various jaunty angles.
There is no bow needed for this basket.

Christmas Variation: Prepare the basket, using German statice instead of baby's breath and dried cranberries or rose hips instead of apples. Adorn the basket handle with a red and green plaid bow.

BREATH OF SUMMER BASKET
Materials:
Drop cloth
Scissors
Glue gun and hot glue sticks
Artemisia
Rose buds
Lavender sprigs (fresh or dried)
Sage sprigs (fresh or dried)
White baby's breath (bleached)
Pink and rose colored strawflowers
Small grapevine or twig basket (6 inch, natural dark or painted)

Instructions:
Spread artemisia around the rim of the basket.
Glue in place with hot glue.
In the artemisia, position and glue rosebuds at regular intervals.
Between the rosebuds position and glue the strawflowers.
Snip any long stems of herbs so the sprigs will be no larger than two inches.
Position and glue the herbs as needed for contrast in color and texture.
Snip small clusters of baby's breath to fill in around the rosebuds and strawflowers.
Glue the baby's breath as needed.

Note: As with the autumn basket, decide whether the design is to be basically baby's breath accented with flowers or flowers accented with baby's breath. This small, delicate basket is just the right size to use up dwindling supplies before searching or spending on more.

SPRING HAS SPRUNG BASKET
Materials:
 Drop cloth
 Glue gun and hot glue
 Scissors
 Eyelet ruffle
 Blue and green plaid or print ribbon (3/4 inch wide)
 Spanish moss
 Artificial English Ivy
 Artificial bird (blue tones and white)
 Yarrow (yellow flat head)
 Yarrow (wild, off white)
 Tansy buttons (yellow)
 Strawflowers (golden, white)
 Lavender flowers
 Blue statice
 German statice (white)
 Baby's breath (natural)
 Willow or other neutral color woven basket

Instructions:
 Spread the drop cloth.
 Arrange supplies of dried materials on the cloth.
 Measure carefully just under the rim the circumference of the basket.
 Cut eyelet ruffle two inches longer than the measurement.
 Glue the ruffle just under the edge of the basket, overlapping at the end.
 Starting where the handle joins the base, with ribbon wrap the basket handle in spiral fashion.
 Cut the ribbon only after wrapping.
 Glue the ribbon at the starting point, rewrap then glue at the finishing point. (This prevents damage to the handle and provides for easy removal if at some point the basket is redecorated.)
 Spread Spanish moss around the rim of the basket.
 Apply glue under the moss to a small area of the rim.
 With gentle pressure hold the moss in place.
 Continue until the entire rim is covered with moss.
 Where the handle joins the rim on the left side (facing you), position and glue the bird.
 Cut three individual ivy leaves from the stem, positioning one leaf under the breast and the others on either side of the tail.
 Glue the leaves around the bird.

Cut ten ivy leaves from the stem and position them in the moss to face outward almost "drooping over" the edge around the rim of the basket.

Group the strawflowers and small lavender head flowers together and glue.

By snipping or breaking, gently separate the flat head yarrow blossom into smaller sections.

Arrange the yarrow and statice (both German and blue) as needed for color.

Add tansy buttons for texture.

Fill in spaces around strawflowers with baby's breath.

Hint: Often on adorned baskets, bows are too much and take away from the delicate beauty of the basket. On this basket, the plaid ribbon bows look best placed where the handles meet the rim. A formal basket adorned with velvet and lace would have the bow at the top.

MINI HERB BASKET
Materials:
Drop cloth
Scissors
Glue gun and hot glue
Small basket (4 to 5 inch diameter)
Tiny-headed baby's breath (gypsophila)
Lavender sprigs
Lavender flower heads
Oregano (flowers and greens)
Sage sprig
Tansy buttons
Yarrow (wild)

Instructions:
Spread materials on drop cloth.

Cut small bunches of baby's breath; each little bunch should be no taller than 1 1/2 inches.

At the starting point on the basket rim apply a generous amount of hot glue (a big glue dot).

Stick two or three small bunches of baby's breath, stems down, in the big glue dot.

Repeat this procedure until the entire rim is covered.

Go around the rim again, applying more glue and more baby's breath achieving a uniform effect.

Using the herbs and flowers sparingly, begin with the lavender sprigs.

Trim each lavender sprig to a length of one inch.

Place a dot of glue on the end of the sprig and gently insert into the baby's breath.

Repeat this so there are six sprigs.

Follow the same procedure of trimming and gluing for the lavender blossoms.

Select sage with small leaves. Remove sage leaves one at a time from the main stem. Place a dot of glue on the tiny leaf and insert deep into the baby's breath.

Add sprigs of oregano and dried oregano blossoms if available.

From now on it is a judgment call from you, the designer:

Is more color needed? Is a wider variety of textures needed? The tansy buttons vary in color from bright gold to warm brown. A small amount of wild yarrow inserted throughout the baby's breath can look good or ruin everything. A bow of any type detracts from the delicacy of this basket.

A BIRD IN THE HEART BASKET
Materials:
> Drop cloth
> Glue gun and hot glue sticks
> Pruning shears
> Scissors
> Medium gage wire
> Wire cutters
> Heart shape basket
> Spanish moss
> Artificial bird with pink and rose tones
> Tiny satin-look, woven edge ribbon (cream, teal and rose colors, 1/8 inch wide)
> Baby's breath (natural color)
> Small pink rose buds
> Rosemary sprigs (dried)
> Sage leaves (dried)
> Thyme sprigs (dried)
> Eucalyptus (2-3 long branches, blue-green)

Instructions:
> Prepare piles of dried materials on the drop cloth.
> If there is a handle on the basket, remove it.
> Begin at the bottom "V" of the heart.
> **Note:** When working with baby's breath or statice, it may be necessary to break up clusters and regroup the stems to make blossom clus-

ters the size and shape you want.

Prepare small bunches of baby's breath about three inches long.

With flower heads pointing towards the "V" glue ONLY THE STEMS to the edge of the basket.

Position the second bunch to overlap, covering the stems of the first bunch, and glue.

Proceed in this manner until you have come full circle, or heart as it is in this case, and the last stems are hidden by the blossoms of the first bunch.

Starting at the point between the two arches of the heart, measure a eucalyptus branch working it around to the "V".

Glue the eucalyptus around the heart just behind the baby's breath border.

Repeat the eucalyptus procedure on the other side of the heart.

Cut off any excess eucalyptus as the branches meet at the "V".

Some individual branches are not long enough to extend from the top to the arch to the "V". if this is the case, fill in with another branch that has the same size leaves.

From Spanish moss prepare a nest for the bird.

Work some small pieces of thyme into the composition of the nest.

Glue the nest in the interior of the heart at the "V".

Glue the bird in the nest so she is peeking out of the heart.

Using three colors of ribbon, make a multi-loop bow with streamers long enough to drape. The size of the bow is determined by the size of the heart.

Glue the bow at the point between the two arches.

As the streamers are draped, separate them so that they drape at different intervals. Glue ribbons in three or four draped positions. Evaluate the overall look and determine how much additional decoration is needed.

Glue a rosebud at the "V".

Working from the "V" space several rosebuds around the heart.

Add rosemary, sage and thyme where needed for color or texture.

Cut a six-inch length wire and prepare a hanging loop by twisting the ends of the wire together.

With hot glue affix the hanging loop to the back of the basket.

Note: If the basket is open weave, omit the glue and maneuver the wire through the weave and create a loop on the back of the basket.

PLANT	POSITIVE	NEGATIVE
Aloe	Affection	Grief
Angelica	Inspiration	*
Basil	Love, good wishes	Hate
Bay	Fame, glory	*
Borage	Courage	Bluntness
Carnation (red)	*	Sad heart
Carnation (striped)	*	Reject, refuse
Chamomile	Patience, humility	*
Clover (red)	Industrious	*
Daisy	Innocence	*
Dandelion	Visionary, oracle	*
Dill	Good cheer	*
Fennel	Endurance	Grief
Geranium (rose)	Preference	*
Geranium (unscented)	*	Fool, folly
Goldenrod	Encouragement	*
Hibiscus	Delicate beauty	*
Honeysuckle	Generosity	*
Hyacinth (blue)	*	Jealousy
Iris	Pure heart, courage	*
Ivy	Fidelity	*
Lavender	Cleanliness	Distrust
Lemon Balm	Sympathy	*
Marigold	*	Grief
Marjoram	Happiness, joy	*
Mint	Virtue, passion	*
Nasturtium	Patriotism	*
Pansy	Happy thoughts	*
Parsley	Festivity	*
Peppermint	Warm, sensitive	*
Rose	Love	*
Rosebud (red)	Purity	*
Rosebud (white)	Girlish innocence	*
Rosebud (yellow)	*	Infidelity
Rosemary	Remembrance	*
Rue	Good health	Sorrow
Sage	Wisdom	*
Spearmint	Sentimental, warm	*
Sweet Woodruff	Humble spirit	*
Tansy	Immortality	Hostility
Thyme	Courage, bravery	*
Violet	Devotion, modesty	*
Yarrow	Health	War
Zinnia	Remembering friends	*

Crafts for Busy Herb Lovers
(These take an hour or less)

NOSEGAY (Tussie-Mussie)

It is a rare instance that a gift by the hand from the heart is not warmly accepted. Gifts of fresh herbs and flowers are suitable for most occasions. As you will recall, in Elizabethan times a little nosegay of fresh herbs and flowers was a matter of necessity for keeping germs and evil spirits away. The meaning of herbs and flowers enhanced or terminated friendships as Victorian friends and lovers sent symbolic nosegays. Before assembling a nosegay, take a moment to learn the language of herbs and flowers (see chart on previous page).

Materials:

1 fresh flower or herb with 4 to 5-inch stem (rose, zinnia, pansy etc.)

Selected sprigs of herb (marjoram, mint, rosemary)

Tansy leaves, geranium leaves or other greenery

Paper doily

Aluminum foil

Ribbon

Floral tape

Instructions:

The flower or herb in the center of the nosegay will determine the sentiment of the gift.

Arrange 4 or 5 sprigs of herbs around the center flower or herb.

Make an outer ring of greenery.

Check over the nosegay not only for the sentiment you wish to convey but also for overall appearance. Adjust the sprigs, add more if necessary.

Gently gather the stems and hold them together by binding floral tape around the stems.

Cut an 8" X 8" square of aluminum foil.

Place a few drops of water in the foil and draw it up around the wrapped stems.

Pinch the foil into a cup position around the stems.

Fold the doily and make two cuts to form an "x" in the center.

Poke foil wrapped stems through the doily opening.

Allowing extra ribbon for streamers, wrap and tie ribbon around the foil under the doily.

Hint: With the nosegay prepare a little card about the language of flowers and the particular sentiment conveyed in this gift. Give for anniversary, bridal shower, birth of a baby, secret pal, hostess gift, party favors etc.

Variation 1: Surprise luncheon or dinner guests with a small nosegay at each place setting and encourage the guests to take the nosegay home. Post the language of flowers in a prominent place and have each guest uncover the secret message in the nosegay. This will certainly break the ice if conversation is slow. To arrange a mini-nosegay in a tiny container, eliminate the paper doily and tie the ribbon around the small vase. Gently bind the stems with string to keep form to the bouquet. Put each nosegay in its ribbon adorned vase to decorate each place setting.

Variation 2: Lovely, aromatic nosegays can be made from dried herbs and flowers. Assemble in the same manner as the fresh, eliminating the aluminum foil and completely wrapping the stems with floral tape.

MAGNETIC PERSONALITY POTPOURRI GIFTS
Materials:

Doll-size straw hat
One 3" x 3" square of nylon netting
1-2 heaping teaspoons Country Girl blend potpourri
1/8-inch ribbon
Glue gun and hot glue
Self-stick magnetic tape

Instructions:

Run ribbon around the crown of the hat and glue into position.

Make a 6-loop bow, position and glue where the crown meets the brim of the hat.

Spread the square of netting and place the potpourri in the center.

Fold the corners towards the center, forming a little package.

Place several dots of glue in the crown of the hat.

Insert the potpourri package, folded side first into the crown.

Press the potpourri package firmly into the crown for 30 seconds.

Bond 1 inch of magnetic tape to the underside (top) of hat brim. This should be enough magnet to hold the hat on the refrigerator, filing cabinet or other metal surface. If more "power" is needed, add another strip of the magnetic tape on the underside bottom of the brim.

POTPOURRI BASKET MAGNET
Materials:
1" x 2" basket
Eyelet ruffle
One 3" x 3" square of nylon net
1 heaping tablespoon of floral scent potpourri
Glue gun and hot glue
Self-stick magnetic tape

Instructions:
Measure a length of eyelet ruffle to go around the outer edge of the basket.
Spread hot glue around the edge and glue the ruffle in place.
Spread the 3" x 3" square and fill with potpourri.
Fold corners to the center, making a packet of potpourri.
Spread glue around the interior and bottom of the little basket.
With the folded edge towards the bottom of the basket, press the potpourri package into the basket.
Hold the package in place and watch for any glue that might ooze through the little gaps in the weave of the basket.
Affix 1 inch of the magnetic strip on a 2" basket side just below the ruffle.
Variation 1: Glue red ribbon (1/8-inch) around the top edge of the ruffle. Fill the little ruffled basket with cinnamon sticks and tiny hemlock cones for holiday tree trim. It can be converted to a magnet by adding the magnetic tape.
Variation 2: Fill these tiny ruffled baskets with individual packages of culinary herbs or bath herbs to decorate each place setting at a birthday luncheon, baby or bridal shower.

BIRD ON THE WING DECORATED BIRD HOUSE
Materials:
Drop cloth
Heavy duty jute (twine for household use)
Scissors
Wire cutters
Lightweight floral wire
Glue gun and hot glue
Bird house
Spanish moss
Greek oregano sprigs
Thyme sprigs
Baby's breath

Red clover (can be used fresh)
Tansy buttons

Instructions:
Place the bird house on the drop cloth.
Work the moss into a mass that will cover the roof of the little house.
Spread the moss mass over the roof to give it a "thatched" look.
Lift portions of moss, spread glue on the exposed roof, gently pat moss back into position.
Starting at the highest point on the roof and working down, posi-

tion fresh Greek oregano leaf "shingles" in a simple pattern. If only dry sprigs are available, run them in a vertical pattern down either side of the roof and glue into position.
Make a miniature swag to drape along the front roof line using the jute for the base.
Measure the roof from eve to top point to the other eve.
Cut the jute six inches longer than the measurement.
Tie a double knot at each end of the jute.
Pull the ends to make a soft fluffy fringe.
Prepare tiny bundles of herbs and clover.
Bind the stems with two wraps of wire.
Using more wire to bind the bundles to the jute, overlap the tiny herb bundles.
When the swag is complete, drape the swag along the eaves of the little bird house holding it in place at the high point of the roof and at the eaves with hot glue.
Cut four 12-inch lengths of jute.
Holding all the lengths as one, tie a shoelace bow.
Adjust the loops but don't cut the streamers until you have decided upon the location of the bow.
Glue the bow to either the perch just below the door opening or at the point of the roof.
Trim the streamers, if they seem too long.
Tie each streamer about one inch from the end.
Separate and fluff the portion of jute below the knot.

DAINTY DOOR BELL
Materials:
   1 oversize sleigh bell (10 to 12 inch circumference)
   16 inches of half-inch rope of bronze/gold colored heavy macrame cord
   Glue gun and hot glue
   Scissors
   4 feet of 3/4-inch print ribbon
   12-14 small branches of tiny-headed baby's breath
   8 oregano flowers, lavender flowers or any small dried blossoms

Instructions:
   Loop the rope; place the free ends against the front of the hanger located on the top of the bell. (Should there be no metal hanger, pile a quantity of hot glue on the center top of the bell. Put both ends of the rope in the glue and hold in place until the glue sets up.)
   Prepare a multi-loop (12-14 loops) bow with no streamers.
   Glue the bow to the rope and the top of the bell.
   Position the tiny-head baby's breath and herbs among the loops.
   Glue everything into position.

   Victorian Variation: Use velvet ribbon and lace for the bow and lavender flowers and sprigs with the natural color baby's breath.
   Christmas Variation: The bells are available in red as well as gold. Use Christmas ribbon, green macrame cord, tiny pine cones, bleached white tiny-head baby's breath, broken cinnamon sticks etc.

BIRD AT REST DECORATION
Materials:
   1 artificial bird
   Nesting material (Spanish moss or silver mound artemisia)
   Sprigs of oregano and rosemary
   Glue gun and hot glue
   1 4-inch embroidery hoop
   1 or 2 colors of 1/8-inch ribbon for a bow and a hanging loop (the length of ribbon will vary according to the size of the bow)
   Walnut stain
   Soft cloth for staining the embroidery hoop
   Newspaper

Instructions:
Spread newspaper and follow the directions on the can for applying the stain to the wooden embroidery hoop.

After the inner and outer hoops are stained, reassemble the hoop with the small hoop at right angle inside the larger hoop.

Glue the two hoops at the top and bottom points where they intersect.

Make a little bird nest of moss and herbs.

Glue the nest inside at the point where the hoops intersect to form the base.

Glue the bird into the nest.

Adorn the top with ribbons and streamers.

Make a hanging loop of ribbon and glue or tie onto the top where the hoops intersect.

Variation: Instead of staining the wooden hoop, wrap it with ribbon and proceed as directed.

HOOPING IT UP POTPOURRI ORNAMENT
Materials:
Lavender scented potpourri
1 4-inch embroidery hoop
1 7-inch square unbleached muslin
1 7-inch square cream colored lace
1 16-inch length of pregathered cream colored lace ruffle
1 18-inch length of 1/8-inch wide lavender colored ribbon
1 18-inch length of 1/8-inch wide cream colored ribbon
1 6-inch length of 1/8-inch wide ribbon (cream or lavender) to use as a ribbon hanger
Glue gun and hot glue
Scissors

Instructions:
Open the embroidery hoop into two separate circles.

Place the muslin square inside the smaller circle so that the edges droop over the sides.

Fill the muslin with potpourri.

Place the lace square on top of the potpourri and muslin.

Spread hot glue in four areas around the inside of the large hoop.

Quickly place the hoop over the lace and muslin squares before the glue begins to set up.

If the embroidery hoop used is the screw type, tighten the screws at this point.

Trim the excess fabric from the edges.

Begin at the top behind the screw and spread hot glue on the back of the hoop's rim, covering about one half of the rim.

Evenly, position the stitched edge of the lace in the glue.

Repeat the gluing process for the second half of the rim. Allow for a 1/4-inch overlap as the ends of the lace meet at the top.

Trim any excess lace.

Make a multi-loop bow with the ribbon.

Tie or glue the bow to the top of the hoop.

Glue the ribbon loop hanger behind the bow.

SCENTED HOT PADS
Materials:

One 9" x 9" panel print square (actual squares vary from print to print)

One 9" x 9" square fabric to correspond with colors in panel print

Polyester filling (for this project the roll is better to use than "bulk fluff." Cotton quilt batting works also)

Sewing machine and thread

Straight pins

Scissors

Fabric glue

3 tablespoons spice scented potpourri

Instructions:

After panel and backing square are cut, place the right sides together and pin.

With straight pins, divide one side of the square (my choice is generally the bottom) into thirds.

Beginning at the one third mark, stitch around the portion of the bottom square as well as the other three sides of the square. Stitch as close to the edge of the fabric as you can.

Stop at the pin mark on the fourth side so that the center one third of the side remains unstitched.

Remove the pins and turn the square "right side" out.

Press the square, making sure to press the raw edges of the unsewn area inward.

If a corner doesn't turn well, seems bulky even after ironing, turn the square inside out and trim the excess off the corner.

Reverse the square and press again.

Cut two 8" x 8" thicknesses of the fiber roll.

Fold both fiber squares in half and insert into the hot pad.

Between the layers spoon in the potpourri.

Spread the spices and herbs around so they are evenly distributed.

Following the fabric glue directions, close the opening.

Hint: Make several spiced hot pads at one time. To retain the aroma keep them sealed in an air-tight plastic bag.

HERB SCENTED MUG MAT
Materials:

1 5" x 5" panel print square

1 5" x 5" fabric square to coordinate with panel print

Polyester filling (the rolled variety)

1 tablespoon potpourri (the scent to match the occasion)

Sewing machine and thread

Straight pins

Scissors

Fabric glue

Instructions:

Follow the directions for making the SCENTED HOT PAD.

Hint: A mug mat, a mug and a packet of herb tea make a thoughtful gift. Keep several on hand for unexpected gift giving occasions such as a thank you, sorry you are sick, just thinking of you etc.

DOLLY DELIGHT DECORATIVE HANGING SACHET
Materials:

1" solid wooden bead

8" x 30" piece of print fabric

1 yard lace (3/4" wide)

1 yard seam binding (a color to accent the print fabric)

12-inch piece of 1/8" wide ribbon in color to accent print fabric

Heart pattern that measures 3 1/2" x 4"

Glue gun and hot glue

Scissors

Needle and thread

Polyester fiber for filling

1 tablespoon potpourri

Spanish moss, excelsior or finely shredded jute

Tiny-head baby's breath and other tiny flowers

Instructions:
The Heart:
Cut one 5" x 20" strip of fabric and set aside.

Cut one 20-inch strip of lace.

Fold remaining fabric to make the heart.

Pin heart pattern on doubled fabric and cut.

Put the right sides of the heart together and stitch around it leaving an opening on one side for the filling.

Turn the heart inside out so the right side is the "out" side and press with a hot iron. While pressing, fold in the raw edges of the opening.

Spoon the potpourri into the opening of the heart.

Pad with polyester filling; plump out the heart.

Close the heart with a thin line of hot glue.

The size of the heart varies from doll to doll so measure around the finished heart before cutting the lace to adorn it. Once the lace is cut, glue it around the back of the heart producing a ruffled effect from the front view.

The Head:
Select moss, excelsior or jute for the hair.

Work the material into a suitable hairstyle. (At this point I discover that the doll's personality is emerging, and I usually end up naming her.)

Glue the hair into place.

Add a small dried herb flower in her hair if you wish.

Glue the head in the space between the two mounds of the heart.
The Body:
Glue a 20-inch strip of lace to the outside edge of the 5" x 20" fabric you cut earlier.

Fold the fabric (right side inside).

Spread a fine line of glue along the raw edge (the 5-inch width) and bond the raw edges together.

Turn fabric to the right side.

Gather the raw edges of the 10-inch side and pin in several places to hold the gathers.

Position the gathers on the back of the heart. (Make sure the seam is running down the back of the skirt.)

Carefully glue the gathered skirt to the heart, removing the pins as you glue.

Wait 5 minutes and check to see that all the gathers "took the glue."

Reapply in areas that didn't hold.

Cut one 10-inch strip of seam binding.

Tie a knot about an inch from each end. The knot looks like a heel, and the end of the seam binding resembles a little foot.

Fold the seam binding legs in half.

Put 1/2 of legs up in the skirt and glue at the fold.

Little legs will hang down from under the skirt.

Cut a 28-inch strip of seam binding.

Fold the seam binding in half.

The loop that is created by the fold will serve as a hanger for the doll. With the doll on her face, position the loop where the skirt is glued to the heart so that four inches of loop extends over her head. As you glue make an "X" with the seam binding. The loose ends will come around the front of the doll as arms. After the "X" is secure, place a dot of glue on the edges of the skirt where the arms come to the front.

Tie knots one inch from the end for the hands just as you did for the feet. If the arms seem too long, trim them.

Prepare a tiny bouquet of baby's breath and herbs.

Tie the bouquet with ribbon.

Have streamers coming from the bouquet if you wish.

Glue the little hands together with the bouquet in them.

Note: Although these directions do not call for features on the doll face, you may add them. My experience with felt tip markers for the features is that the color frequently spreads into the wood grain. I prefer permanent marking pens with the very fine line point.

*"I will arise and go now, and go to Innisfree.
And a small cabin build there, of clay and wattles made:
And nine bean-rows will I have there, and a hive for the
honey bee,
And live alone in the bee-loud glade."*

The Lake Isle of Innisfree
William Butler Yeats

MY BLUE HEAVEN ANGEL SACHET
Materials:
   One 1-inch wooden bead
   30 inches of 4-inch blue paper twist ribbon
   5" x 10" print fabric
   12 inches of 1/8-inch ribbon
   14 inches of 1-inch lace
   Polyester filling
   Spanish moss, excelsior, or finely shredded jute
   1 tablespoon potpourri

Needle and thread
3 1/2" x 4" heart pattern
Straight pins
Scissors
Florist wire
Wire cutters
Glue gun and hot glue

Instructions:
Refer to Dolly Delight Sachet directions for cutting and assembling the heart.
Again refer to Dolly Delight Sachet for preparing and gluing the head to the heart.
Arrange the hair with a bow or dried herbs to decorate.
Glue a small bow to the point of the heart or at the neck.
The Body:
Spread open the paper ribbon, smoothing it, extending it to its full width
Fold the paper ribbon in half.
At approximately the 8 inch mark, cross one strip over the other to make an "X."
There will be a loop at the top.
Find the center of the loop and bring it to the point behind the "X."
Pinch the "X" and the loop to form a bow.
Run floral wire around the paper ribbon to secure the bow.
Before cutting the wire, make sure enough length is left to make a hanger.
Glue the finished heart with the head attached to the bow.
Work with the loops to position wings for the angel.
With several small dots of glue join the two strips to form a skirt.
Trim the finished skirt to a desirable length.
Hint: Use the small ribbon as a decorative hanger instead of the floral wire.

PANDORA'S SURPRISE STRAW BOX
Materials:
4-inch circular straw box with lid
Cream color ruffled eyelet
Glue gun and hot glue sticks
Scissors
Spanish moss
Lavender sprigs

Sage leaves
3 rosebuds
Tiny-headed baby's breath (natural color)

Instructions:
Do not cut the ruffle until the distance around the top edge of the box is measured, providing a 1/2-inch overlap.

Cut ruffle and position it so that the edge of the ruffle meets the edge of the box top.

Glue the ruffle to the lid.

Arrange the Spanish moss on the lid, working it out from the center to cover the glued edge of the ruffle.

Glue the three rosebuds in the center of the moss.

Stick sprigs of lavender in the moss to give a "spokes of a wheel" effect as the lavender comes out from the center rosebuds.

Carefully remove the dry sage leaf from the stem.

Position and glue individual sage leaves around the rosebuds.

Fill in the spaces with the tiny-headed baby's breath.

Hint: The number of uses for this box is only limited by your imagination. If you use the box for herb scented powder, place the powder in a closed plastic bag before putting it in the box.

Variation: Use a 3-inch or smaller straw box decorated in the same fashion and the 4-inch box using silver mound artemisia, one straw flower, rosemary sprigs, and tiny-headed baby's breath.

HERB DECORATED CANDLES
Materials:
1 "store bought" candle
"Wilted" but not completely dry tansy leaves, rose petals, sage leaves, oregano leaves etc.
3 Tablespoons of white glue
1-2 teaspoons of water
Measuring spoons
Paint brush
Waxed paper
Aluminum pie pan
Disposable plastic container

Instructions:
Measure the white glue into a plastic container.

Add water a few drops at a time to thin the glue; (the glue should be a creamy consistency but not watery).

Cut small pieces of waxed paper, one for each herb or leaf to be used.

Carefully paint the herb or leaf with white glue.

Pick up the paper with the herb on it, applying even pressure. Affix the herb or leaf to the candle.

Remove the waxed paper backing.

At this point you have the option of adjusting or smoothing.

With your forefinger gently apply pressure to the area in question.

Add other herbs and leaves if you want a design rather than a single spray

Set the candle aside to dry (approximately 30 minutes).

Cover the glue container until it is time to "glue-paint" the entire surface of the candle.

Add three tablespoons of white glue to the container and thin as suggested above.

Place the candle in the aluminum pan and holding the candle by the wick, "glue paint" the candle. With nice even strokes beginning at the top of the candle and working to the bottom, paint one half of the candle.

Carefully turn the candle and proceed the same way covering the remaining area with thinned white glue.

Note: You may wish to repeat the coating process. Let the candle dry two hours, so the surface is not sticky to the touch, before another painting. Humidity does influence drying time.

Variation 1: Use a 12-inch or larger taper candle and affix a spiral pattern of oregano around it.

Variation 2: For favors at a bridal luncheon, baby shower, or as a surprise for a group of friends "doing lunch" select votive candles in colors to accent the color theme and decorate with herbs. Place the decorated votive candles in foil cupcake liner papers at each place.

HERB SCENTED CANDLE USING ESSENTIAL OIL
Materials:
Household paraffin
Lavender essential oil
Purple crayon
Double boiler

Candle wick
Pencil or meat skewer
Newspaper
Paint stick or some type of disposable stick for stirring the hot paraffin
1 quart milk container cut in half or a clean soup can with one end removed
1 tablespoon cooking oil for lubricating the metal mold

Instructions:
Spread out several layers of newspaper on the work surface.
If using the can for a mold, lubricate the interior sides and bottom of the can with cooking oil.
Dangle the wick inside the can or milk carton to measure the amount of wick you will need. Measure and cut amount of wick needed for the candle allowing an extra two inches to tie around the pencil or meat skewer.
Rest the pencil or skewer with the wick attached on the edges of the can or carton.
Fill bottom half of double boiler with water.
Heat on high until the water comes to a boil. (Keep the heat high enough so the water continues a slow boil. Keep checking the amount of water so the pan does not boil dry.)
Place the top of the double boiler over the hot water and add one slab. (Breaking the paraffin into several pieces will make it melt faster.)
CAUTION: DO NOT LEAVE PARAFFIN UNATTENDED ON THE STOVE. NOT ONLY WILL IT BURN SKIN; HOT PARAFFIN IS ALSO FLAMMABLE IF ALLOWED TO OVERHEAT.
Peel the crayon and stir one quarter of it into the melting paraffin.
As one slab of paraffin melts, add a second slab.
Add more purple if a deeper lavender is desired.
After the paraffin is melted, stir in four drops of lavender essential oil.
Carefully pour the hot paraffin into the candle mold, reserving about one fourth cup melted paraffin.
CAUTION: DO NOT HOLD THE MOLD WITH ONE HAND AND POUR WITH THE OTHER. KEEP BOTH HANDS ON THE POT HANDLE. THE CANDLE MOLD IS ON A THICKNESS OF NEWSPAPERS AND DRIPPING PARAFFIN WILL NOT HURT ANYTHING.
Be prepared to see an indentation forming around the wick as the

candle cools. This is normal. Pour additional melted wax to fill up the indentation. When the candle is completely cold and set up, remove it from the mold by either tearing away the paper of the milk carton or by means of a can opener cutting the other end out of the can and pushing the candle through.

Hint: If for some reason the candle is difficult to remove from the metal mold, simply heat water and, holding the candle by the wick, slosh it up and down several times. Remove the candle from the water and push again from the open bottom.

Note: If any wax is unused, pour it into a metal container for use as pinecone fire starter base.

Variation: Once again let the creative ideas flow. You may add a single scent or a combination of scents. This is a great way to recycle the bits and pieces of crayons rejected by the family "artists." The coloring for your original candle is limited only by your crayon supply.

Cleaning the paraffin pan

After all the wax has been used, place the pan back on top of the double boiler. The heat will keep the paraffin from setting up. With a paper towel or thickness of newspaper, wipe out the inside of the pan. You may need to repeat this procedure several times to remove all the wax. Wash in hot sudsy water. As you dry the pan, you will be able to tell if there is any residue left. If so, just heat, wipe and wash again.

CANDLES MADE FROM FRESH HERBS
Materials:
Paraffin
5 sprigs of fresh lemon thyme
One 16-ounce can
Candle wick
Yellow crayon (optional)
Vegetable oil
Newspaper
Pencil or meat skewer
Double boiler

Instructions:
Follow the directions, the candle mold preparations and the cautions for making an herb-scented candle with essential oil. Rather than add essential oil, snip the stems of the lemon thyme into 1/2-inch lengths.

Stir in the lemon thyme just before pouring the melted paraffin into the mold.

Reserve 1/4 cup of melted paraffin to fill the indentation that forms around the wick as the candle cools.

Store extra wax and clean pan as directed in making an herb-scented candle with essential oil.

Variation: Stir three drops cinnamon oil into the hot wax. Instead of fresh herb, drop 24 whole cloves one at a time and 3 cinnamon sticks broken into small slivers into the wax as it is setting up in the mold.

HERB SCENTED CANDLE WITH POWDERED HERBS
Materials:
 4 slabs of paraffin
 Powdered oregano, sage or rosemary
 Candle wick
 Half gallon milk container (cardboard) or 16 ounce tin can
 Pencil or meat skewer
 Newspaper
 Double boiler
 Paint stir stick

Instructions:
Cut approximately 1/3 off the top of the milk container if this is to be the candle mold. Refer to the directions and cautions for making an herb-scented candle with essential oil.

To have a uniformly colored candle, stir in amount of powdered herb to color and scent the wax to your satisfaction and pour immediately into the mold.

Some of the herb will settle to the bottom.

Five minutes after the wax has been poured into the mold, protect your hand with a pot holder, grasp the mold in the protected hand and stir three times.

Sprinkle one teaspoon of powdered herb on the top.

Fill in the indentation with wax containing powdered herb.

Tap the exterior of the mold three times.

Hint: The surface of the candle may not be smooth when it is removed from the mold. Heat water to the simmer point (just under a boil) and holding the candle by the wick slosh it up and down in the hot water. Ridges, grooves and small surface flaws will "melt away."

Variation: Add mint leaves and peppermint essential oil.

LAYERED HERB SCENTED CANDLE USING POWDERED HERBS
Materials:
 4 slabs of paraffin

Powdered herb (basil, thyme or oregano for green, ground ginger for gold, paprika for red tones)
1/2-gallon cardboard milk carton for candle mold
Candle wick
Pencil or meat skewer
Newspapers
Double boiler

Instructions:
Spread a thickness of newspaper.

Prepare the candle mold by cutting off the top of the milk carton, leaving as much of the straight sides as possible.

Melt one slab of paraffin in the top of the double boiler.

Stir in 1 tablespoon of powdered herb.

Pour the herb paraffin mixture into the mold and set it aside until the wax is firm. To speed the firming process, put the carton in the refrigerator.

Melt another slab of paraffin and add 2 teaspoons of powdered herb.

Again, let the layer firm up before adding additional layers.

Repeat the process using 1 teaspoon powdered herb for the third layer.

Melt the final slab of paraffin and without adding any herb pour it into the mold, reserving a small amount to fill the indentation that will form as the candle cools.

After the candle is completely cool, tear away the cardboard mold.

Variation 1: Using a quart-size milk carton, following the instructions for the half-gallon candle, repeat the process a second time to create a tall eight layer candle.

Variation 2: To make a multi-color candle, alternate layers of different herbs. Wipe out the top of the double boiler after each melting so the colors won't carry over from one layer to the next.

PINE CONE FIRE STARTERS
Materials:
Shallow tin cans (6 1/8 oz. or 10 oz.)
Pine cones
Paraffin, candle stubs, leftover herb scented paraffin
Wax crayons (green, red and gold)
Double boiler
Wooden paint stick
Newspapers

Instructions:

Spread several layers of newspaper on the work surface.

Place one pine cone in each can to assure fit.

Remove cone from can and place on paper next to the can.

Melt paraffin in the top of the double boiler.

Using the wooden paint stick to stir the melt-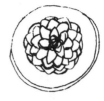
ing paraffin, add bits of peeled crayon for color.

Observing all candle-making cautions, pour
approximately one inch of melted paraffin into
each can.

Put each pine cone in the paraffin.

Let cool.

To remove the pine cone nested in paraffin, heat a pan of water to
the boiling point. Take the pan from the heat. With a potholder or
tongs grasp each can at the top rim.

Dip the can half way into the hot water and hold to the count of
five. Grasp the top of the pine cone and with a gentle turning motion
pull it from the can. If the cone is not released, repeat the procedure.

PET PLEASING PRESENTS
CATNIP KITTIES

Materials:

Catnip (available in dry form at pet shops and pet care departments. It is easy to grow, too.)

3 lengths of 5" x 10" print fabric

Kitty pattern

Yarn

Small bells

Large bell

18-inch length of burlap ribbon

Scissors

Straight pins

Sewing machine and thread

Standard needle and thread

Large eye tapestry needle

Instructions:

Fold fabric with right sides facing.

Draw a free-hand pattern or trace the pattern from this book.

Pin pattern on folded fabric.

Still with right sides of fabric together, stitch around the edge of
the kitty leaving a 1-inch opening at the bottom.

Trim the edges around the tail, coming as close as possible to the stitching.

Turn the kitty right side out.

Use a pen top (not the point with ink!) to help work the curved tail into position.

Fill the kitty with catnip.

By hand stitching, close the hole (while fabric glue and other bonding agents would be quicker and are said to be harmless to animals, why subject pets to any unnecessary chemicals?)

Cut one 12-inch length of yarn and thread two small bells on it.

Double the yarn and tie it tightly around the catnip kitty's neck, making a double knot to hold the yarn.

About half way down the lengths of yarn, knot the strings. Fringe and fluff out the yarn under the knots.

Using the directions, make 2 additional kitties.

Cut three 10-inch lengths of yarn.

Knot the starting end.

Braid the lengths and tie at the other end.

Measure and glue (use hot glue) a 3 inch loop at one end of the burlap ribbon

Run the yarn braid through the loop.

Knot the braid to form a hanging loop.

Cut a 30-inch length of yarn.

Thread the tapestry needle with the yarn.

Decide where on the burlap ribbon to attach the three kitties.

Position the first kitty; with the threaded tapestry needle start on the front of the burlap beside the kitty and run the thread to the underside leaving about a 4 inch length of yarn.

Bring the yarn back through the burlap to the other side of the kitty.

Cut the yarn leaving a 4 to 5 inch length.

Tie a little bow around the kitty's middle to hold it to the burlap.

"Belt" the other kitties to the burlap in this manner.

Cut the lower end of the burlap ribbon in a point.

With the tapestry needle and thread stitch the large bell at the point.

Variation: Stitch 3" x 3" squares and fill with catnip. Run a needle and thread through the center of the filled square, securely stitching a bell to the center of each side of the pillow.

DOGGIE DELIGHT WREATH
Materials:

One 10-inch hard foam wreath base

Solid color 2-inch width ribbon

Five 4-inch calico print bags

Dry herbs for herbal dog rinse

Doggie biscuits, rawhide bone etc.

U pins

Scissors

Rubber cement

Instructions:

Wrap the wreath, overlap style, with the ribbon.

Glue the exposed end of the ribbon.

Make a double loop bow and with the U pin, affix it to the wreath.

Fill the little bags with doggie bath herbs and tie securely.

Place a U pin over the narrow area where the bag is gathered.

With firm even pressure pin the bag to the wreath.

Position the other bags around the wreath and affix in the same manner.

Before you tie a bow around each doggie treat you plan to use (the variety and amount are up to you as you design the wreath) poke a U pin through the ribbon.

After the bow is tied, press the pin (under the treat) into the wreath base.

Repeat until the wreath is decorated to your satisfaction.

Hint: In one of the herbal rinse bags include instructions on how to infuse the herbs to make the rinse.

*"In the presence of nature, a wild delight
runs through a man."*

Nature
Ralph Waldo Emerson

Suggested Reading

Bacon, Richard M. *The Forgotten Arts: Growing, Gardening and Cooking with Herbs.* Dublin, NH: Yankee, Inc., 1972

Bennett, Jennifer. *Lilies of the Hearth.* Camden East, Ontario, Canada: Camden House Publishing, 1991

Fox, Helen Morgenthau. *Gardening with Herbs for Flavor and Fragrance.* New York: Dover Publications, Inc., 1970

Gaden, Eileen. *Biblical Garden Cookery.* Chappaqua, NY: Christian Herald Books, 1976

Gordon, Lesley. *Green Magic.* Exeter, England: Edbury Press, 1977

Johnson, Mary Elizabeth and Pearson, Katherine. *Nature Crafts.* Birmingham, AL: Oxmoor House, Inc., 1980

Kowalchik, Claire and Hylton, William H., eds. *Rodale's Illustrated Encyclopedia of Herbs.* Emmaus. PA: Rodale Press, 1987

Lathrop, Norma Jean. *Herbs: How to Select, Grow and Enjoy.* Tucson, AZ: HP Books, Inc., 1981

Lust, John. *The Herb Book.* New York, NY: Bantam Books, 1974

Michael, Pamela. *All Good Things Around Us.* New York, NY: Sterling Publishing Co., Inc., 1983

Mierhof, Annette. *The Dried Flower Book.* New York, NY: E.P. Dutton, 1981

Oster, Maggie. *Gifts and Crafts from the Garden.* Emmaus, PA: Rodale Press, 1988

Petelin, Carol. *The Creative Guide to Dried Flowers.* Exeter, England: Webb and Bower, Ltd., 1988

Rosengarten, Frederick Jr. *The Book of Spices.* New York, NY: Jove Publications, Inc., 1973

Sanecki, Kay N. *The Book of Herbs.* Seacaucus, NJ: Chartwell Books, Inc., 1985

Simmons, Adelma Grenier. *Country Wreaths from Caprilands.* New York, NY: E.P. Dutton, 1964

Simmons, Adelma Grenier. *Herb Gardening in Five Seasons.* Emmaus, PA: Rodale Press, 1989

Svinicki, Eunice. *Flowercraft.* Racine, WI: Whitman Publishing Co. Inc., 1977

Resources

Herb Gardens for Viewing in the Mid-Atlantic and Southeastern United States

District of Columbia

WASHINGTON CATHEDRAL
Mount Saint Alban
Washington, DC 20016
(202) 537-8982
The Bishop's Garden
An area of historic focus includes emphasis on 11th and 12th Century design.
Open daily.
Admission is free

THE NATIONAL ARBORETUM
This large herb garden, designed and sponsored by The Herb Society of America, is actually 10 smaller theme gardens. Along with culinary and other herb gardens, there is a garden featuring herbal dye plants. There is also a garden dedicated to Dioscorides, the 1st Century Greek physician.
Call ahead for hours of operation.
Admission is free.

Florida

FLORIDA STATE UNIVERSITY
College of Pharmacy
Gainesville
Maintained by the university's College of Pharmacy, this herb garden features medicinal plants and medicinal herbs.
Open to the public all year round.
Admission is free.

Georgia

PINE MOUNTAIN
Callaway Gardens
Nearly eight acres of garden features culinary herbs and vegetables.

Open daily.
Admission is free.

North Carolina
CHAPEL HILL
North Carolina Botanical Garden
University of North Carolina
Laurel Hill Road
Open daily, year round.
Call ahead for information, hours of operation etc.
Admission is free.

DURHAM
Duke Homestead Historic Site
Edna Lovelace Gaston
2828 Duke Homestead Road
Durham, NC 27706
(919) 477-5498
Call ahead for hours of operation.
Group reservations required.

GODWIN
Rasland Farm
The Tippett Family
NC 82 at US 13
Godwin, NC 28344
(919) 567-2705
Annual Herb festival the first weekend in June.
Gardens open May through September.
Guided group tours available by advance reservation.
Admission is free.

MANTEO
The Elizabethan Gardens
Roanoke Island
Created and maintained by The Garden Club of North Carolina.
Emphasis on Elizabethan period and dedicated to the memory of
the members of the "lost" colony of 1585.
Call ahead for information.

South Carolina
CHARLESTON
The Heyward Washington House

87 Church Street
Seasonal tours.
Call for information.

Virginia

CHARLOTTESVILLE
Monticello (Thomas Jefferson's home)
Tours are offered four times a day in summer and twice a day in spring and fall.
Admission is charged.
For tour information write:
Monticello
P.O. Box 316
Charlottesville, VA 22902
(804) 293-2158

MT. VERNON (George Washington's Home)
Mt. Vernon Memorial Highway
Fairfax County
Traditional colonial kitchen herb and vegetable garden.
Sponsored by the Mt. Vernon Ladies' Association.
Open daily, year round.
Admission is charged.

WILLIAMSBURG
John Blair House Herb Garden
Duke of Gloucester Street
Maintained by the Colonial Williamsburg Foundation.
Open daily, year round.
Admission is free.

The George Wythe House
Location: Facing the Palace Green
Maintained by the Colonial Williamsburg Foundation.
Open daily 9 to 5, year round.
Admission by Colonial Williamsburg tour ticket.

West Virginia

BERKELEY SPRINGS
Wrenwood of Berkeley Springs
Flora Hackimer
Rt. 4, Box 361
Berkeley Springs, WV 25411

Garden open year round.
Call ahead for hours of operation.
Admission is free.

Herb Societies and Associations

American Herb Association
P.O. Box 353
Rescue, CA 95672
(916) 626-5046

The Herb Society of America
9019 Kirtland-Chardon Rd.
Mentor, OH 44060
(216) 256-0514

North Carolina Herb Association
Route 1, Box 65
Godwin, NC 28344

Savory Society of Hilton Head
6 Wood Thrush
Hilton Head Island, SC 29928
(803) 681-2537

Where to find it

Where you can find herb plants, seeds, dried herbs and flowers, craft supplies and down-to-earth, friendly advice.

District of Columbia
The Herb Cottage
Washington National Cathedral
Mount Saint Alban
Washington, DC 20016
(202) 537-8982
Herb plants and seeds.

Virginia

Antique Orchard Herbary
Linda Baltimore Morgan
Box 734
Abingdon, VA 24210
Herb tea parties and buffets by reservation.
Gift shop.
Catalog $1.00.

Buffalo Springs Herb Farm
Don Haynie and Tom Hamlin
Raphine, VA
(703) 348-1083
Dried herbs, herbal arrangements and gifts etc.
Gift shop operates in a restored 18th-Century farmhouse.

Heartfelt Farms
Cheryl Taylor
P.O. Box 1513
Salem, VA 24153
Dried herbs, spices, potpourri blends, wreaths, herbal gifts.

Tom Thumb Workshops
Grace Wakefield
Route # 13
P.O. Box 357
Mappsville, VA 23407
(804) 824-3507
Herbs, potpourri, craft supplies, books etc.
Catalog $1.00.

Williamsburg Pottery Factory and Greenhouse
Route 60
Lightfoot, VA 23185
(804) 564-3326
Fresh plants, potpourri and craft supplies.
Open daily until dark, year round.

North Carolina

Gourmet Gardens and Herb Farm
Diane and Dick Weaver
14 Banks Town Road
Weaverville, NC 28787

(704) 865-0766
Herbs, gifts, supplies.
Retail shop.

The Sandy Mush Herb Nursery
Kate and Fairman Jayne
Route 2, Surrett Cove Road
Leicester, NC 28748
(704) 683-2014
Herb plants, seeds, supplies, books etc.
Catalog $4.00.

Rasland Farm
The Tippett Family
Route 1, Box 65
NC 82 at US 13
Godwin, NC 28344
(919) 567-2705
Herb plants, herbal craft supplies, gifts, books etc.
Retail shop.
Catalog $2.50.

Shelton Herb Farm
Margaret Shelton
Route 5, Box 499
Goodman Road
Leland, NC 28451
(919) 253-5964
Herbs, gifts, crafts, supplies etc.
Retail Shop.

South Carolina
Pete's Plant Farm
5920 Chisolm Rd.
Johns Island, SC
(803) 559-1446
Fresh herbs and plants.

Stacy's Garden Greenhouse, Garden Center and Nursery
Highway 321 N
York, SC 29745
(803) 684-2331
Herb plants, books, potpourri supplies and other craft materials.

West Virginia
Wrenwood of Berkeley Springs
Flora Hackimer
Route 4, Box 361
Berkeley Springs
(304) 258-3071
Herb plants, gifts and supplies.
Retail shop.
Catalog $2.00.

National Sources
Aphrodisia
48 Washington Street
Brooklyn, NY 11222
(718) 852-1278
Individual botanicals available or will blend to order, vast array of
essential oils.
Write for catalog.

Balsam Fir Products
Wendy J Newmeyer
P.O. Box 123
West Paris, ME 04289
(207) 674-2094
Balsam products, potpourri, pine cones and other items.

Caprilands Herb Farm
Silver Street
North Coventry, CT 06238
(203) 742-7244
Fresh plants, dried herbs, gifts, books, craft supplies.
Retail Shop.
Catalog sales.

Fox Hill Farm
444 W. Michigan Ave., Box 7
Parma, MI 49269
Excellent source for scented geranium plants.
Many varieties of herbs.
Retail shop and public herb garden.

Write for catalog.

Golden Meadows Herb Farm and Emporium
431 South St. Augustine
Dallas, TX 75217
(214) 398-3479
Live herb plants, dried herbs, teas, oils and books.
Catalog $2.00.

Homestead Herbs
P.O. Box 397
Chester, CA 96020
(916) 596-3628
Dried herbs and spices, herb teas, gift items.
Write for catalog.

The Thyme Garden
20546 Alsea Highway
Alsea, OR 97324
(503) 487-8671.
Popular, difficult to find and exotic herb seeds.
Catalog $1.50.

San Francisco Herb Company
250 14th Street
San Francisco, CA 94103
(415) 816-7174
Dry culinary herbs, spices, botanicals, essential oils and teas.
Write for catalog.

Well-Sweep Herb Farm
317 Mt. Bethel Road
Port Murray, NJ 07865
(908) 852-5390
Herb plants, dried flowers, gifts.
Retail shop.
Catalog $2.00.